Teacher's Resource Book 5

NELSON ENGLISH

John Jackman and Wendy Wren

Contents

Nelson

Nelson English Components

UK Curriculum Coverage

Age range	Skills track	Development track	Teacher's resource books	NC Level	5–14 Level	NIC Level
Foundation 5-7 years	SKILLS FOUNDATION BOOK	DEVELOPMENT FOUNDATION BOOK	TEACHER'S RESOURCE FOUNDATION BOOK	1/2	A/B	1/2
Book 1 7-8 years	SKILLS BOOK 1	DEVELOPMENT BOOK 1	TEACHER'S RESOURCE BOOK 1	3	B	3
Book 2 8-9 years	SKILLS BOOK 2	DEVELOPMENT BOOK 2	TEACHER'S RESOURCE BOOK 2	3/4	B/C	3/4
Book 3 9-10 years	SKILLS BOOK 3	DEVELOPMENT BOOK 3	TEACHER'S RESOURCE BOOK 3	4	C	4
Book 4 10-11 years	SKILLS BOOK 4	DEVELOPMENT BOOK 4	TEACHER'S RESOURCE BOOK 4	4/5	D	4/5
Book 5 11-12 years	SKILLS BOOK 5	DEVELOPMENT BOOK 5	TEACHER'S RESOURCE BOOK 5	5	D/E	5

Introduction to Nelson English

What is Nelson English?

Nelson English is a twin-track course which aims to provide an underpinning structure to the teaching of English for key stages 1 and 2 (England, Wales and Northern Ireland) and levels A–D/E (Scotland), focusing particularly on the knowledge, skills and understanding of writing. Throughout the course reading, listening and speaking opportunities are built in at all levels. **Nelson English (NE)** is also suitable for those older pupils who need more support.

The basic skills (including punctuation, grammar, spelling etc.) are mainly tackled within the **Skills** track while the conceptual skills relating to the craft of writing are the stuff of the **Development** track. In the **Skills** track the material tends to be more skills focused but still within a context. In the **Development** track the material tends to be more developmental or meaning based, but again, not without skills. You simply can't have one without the other.

Nelson English recognises the richness and range of good practice in most schools, and provides a systematic progression to enable young writers to acquire and develop the skills necessary to realise their full potential.

Any craft, including good functional, personal and imaginative writing, requires key skills and knowledge. Whilst recognising that there are many different approaches and attitudes to the teaching of English, **NE** provides teaching materials that can offer a graded progression to the acquisition of basic skills and understanding of language.

Nelson English seeks, unambiguously, to help to teach the skills of English and to provide the young writer with the 'tools of the trade'. These go beyond simply covering the predictable rules of punctuation, grammar, spelling, vocabulary etc., important as these are. The course also identifies as skills those strategies which are required to 'write for varied purposes ... for an extended range of readers ... [understand] the characteristics of different kinds of writing'. *(English in the National Curriculum (1995).)* **NE** addresses these concepts, supplying pupils with learning opportunities to facilitate well-constructed plot and character creation, as well as opportunities for planning, drafting and improving their work. By using throughout a wide range of carefully selected stimulus material, the course provides opportunities to work in the full range of genres appropriate to the children's interests, and complementary to other curriculum requirements.

What does Nelson English comprise?

Nelson English begins at **Foundation Level** with a **Skills Big Book** supported by three **Skills Workbooks** and a **pupils' book**. (The workbook material is also available as copymasters in the **Teacher's Resource Book**.) The parallel **Development** track comprises a **pupils' book** which ties in with the **Skills** track materials or can stand alone if required.

The **Foundation Level** is followed by five further levels, each comprising a **pupils' book** in each track. The **pupils' books** contain a number of teaching units: most units are four or six pages in extent, and each might be expected to provide the English work for an average child for about a week. The material is so sequenced that the units from the two tracks complement each other, and may be used together – either with the whole class, with groups or with individual children. However the tracks are carefully devised to stand alone if required.

All English teaching requires a context, and **NE** has focused on the themes which research in many schools has indicated are consistently used by many teachers. These themes provide a purposeful context in both tracks on which the underpinning English work is built. Pupils will perhaps have had previous exposure to the themes used, will currently be working on them, or this course will serve as an introduction to forthcoming work in other curricular areas. But whatever the circumstances in each particular classroom, the context is essentially secondary to the core English teaching for which the books are designed.

The pupils' material is supported and extended by a **Teacher's Resource Book** at each level. These books contain extensive photocopiable material devised to help children who need additional support and consolidation. Some of these photocopy masters also provide extension activities. These books give the answers to the **pupils' book** exercises where appropriate.

How should Nelson English be used?

Different schools will have different approaches, so methods of usage will differ, but the course has been planned from the outset for maximum flexibility of use.

- Providing the 'essential diet', **NE** can be used as a comprehensive, stand-alone English course.
- The tracks can be used in parallel, with pupils in a class working on complementary units across both tracks. Alternatively, the tracks may be followed sequentially or even independently from each other.
- Many schools will want their pupils to work through much of **NE** independently and at their own pace, but the books are written assuming a degree of teacher intervention and support if the most effective use is to be made of the ideas and material offered. Attention to page design at an early stage has resulted in an accessible and inviting layout to children.
- As a rich resource, **NE** might be dipped into, to reinforce the work of the whole class or individuals as required.
- As a complement to cross-curricular topic work, **NE** will deepen and extend the opportunities for language work.
- At **Foundation Level,** the school may elect either to adopt the **Workbooks** to support the skills introduced in the **Skills Big Book,** or teachers may opt to photocopy this material from the accompanying **Teacher's Resource Book.**

Teachers who choose to use **NE** as a dip-in resource or to use the **Development** track alone, are advised that certain required skills are introduced in the **Skills** track, such as the use of a dictionary in **Skills Book** 2. For this reason teachers not using the **Skills** track, or who are working through **NE** in their own order, will need to teach these skills to enable their pupils to tackle confidently some of the work given in the **Development** track.

How is Nelson English assessed?

Assessment and record keeping provision is an important component of the materials. Frequent revision and testing of the skills in the pupils' books is supported by copiable records of pupils' progress. These provide opportunities for teachers to constantly, but conveniently, monitor and estimate progress and attainment. There is a simple but comprehensive record sheet for each book, so there are two sheets at each level.

The record sheets (see pages 118 – 119) may be produced in duplicate as it can be a positive incentive for the children to complete their own copies as they tackle the activities in **Nelson English**.

Teachers may choose to make work storage folders from their own more elaborately completed record sheets, enabling them to keep selected samples of work from exercises in the **Development** track, together with the sheets of paper on which the **Skills** track *Check-ups* were undertaken. This simple strategy conveniently provides the necessary profiling evidence required to demonstrate understanding and progress in the skills and concepts learnt as the child progresses through the carefully graded course.

During the development of this course, some schools experimented with pupil self-assessment, and this has been found a useful activity in a number of cases. Some teachers constructed simple questionnaires for their pupils to answer at various stages. It is important, however, that self-assessment by pupils of this age should always be a positive activity, steering them to indicate what has been enjoyed and where success has been realised, rather than where failure has been experienced. Suitably worded leading questions, in which children might admit to a lower 'enjoyment rating', can often lead the alert teacher to realise that the lack of enjoyment in undertaking a particular task might well be the result of lack of understanding. We have not, therefore, provided specific self-assessment sheets, but the record sheets have been designed to enable pupils to use them too, if so desired.

How does Nelson English relate to the statutory national curricula?

As is clear from the correlation charts and scope and sequence charts which appear on the following pages, **Nelson English** has been produced to meet the essential requirements of the curricula currently in use throughout the United Kingdom. Where these requirements differ the material errs in favour of introducing skills or concepts sooner rather than later. In order to ensure adequate consolidation prior to assessment, the teaching of most skills and concepts is introduced, at an appropriate level of understanding, as early as possible.

How is the work in Nelson English sequenced?

As with course materials in other subjects, such as mathematics, new skills and concepts are introduced slowly and progressively. Starting with a firm foundation of the requirements for the youngest age groups, the material in all its facets is progressive and repetitive. It is never assumed that a concept has been mastered or internalised simply because it has been introduced before. Opportunities are constantly offered for reinforcement and revision, and when related skills and concepts are being introduced the activities are designed to allow for the earlier material to be revisited.

However, **Nelson English** seeks neither to over-estimate the potential of the young writer, nor to be condescending. Whilst being careful to present material at a stage and in a manner accessible to the majority of pupils, the authors believe that within their individual limitations most children prefer to be tested and stretched.

The Scope and Sequence charts which appear on pages 12 – 17, 19 – 22, 23 and 87 summarise the content of the whole course in general and the content of the two Books 5 in detail, and illustrate where a skill or concept is initially introduced and where and how frequently it is returned to in the pupils' books.

Where and when to introduce new skills and concepts has been carefully planned. Draft materials have been tested with the project trial schools, some of which integrated the framework into their curriculum plans whilst the project was still in preparation, which has benefited the programme.

Local knowledge and the experience of teachers will quite properly suggest different regimes for approaching the teaching of English, both from child to child and from school to school. Also much will depend on the style and approach of English teaching to which a child has previously been exposed. Evidence has shown that children who have not been accustomed or expected to apply themselves to more structured English tasks are soon able and happy to apply themselves productively to this type of work, alongside the equally important freer language work which exists in all good classrooms.

The structure and sequencing of **Nelson English** is intended to *support* not *supplant* existing good practice.

Introduction to Skills Book 5 and Development Book 5

Most children coming to these books will have had exposure to the earlier levels of the **Nelson English** course. For these children most of the concepts and skills taught in the books will be familiar, and will provide essential on-going practice and consolidation.

To this end the **pcms** in the Skills track at this level may be collected together, as is indicated by **pcm** 1 in **Skills Unit** 1, and used as a complete revision guide to the key skills of punctuation, grammar and spelling.

For other children these two books will be their first encounter with structured language work of this sort, so not only will the content be new to them, but the method of working will also require careful introduction. However experience has shown that most children enjoy, and soon get considerable satisfaction from, progressing through such a course.

Teachers will use their own experience to determine whether or when to arrange for some of the work to be conducted in groups. Generally, at the specific request of teachers who helped with the development of this course, the material assumes children will be working individually and independently. Opportunities for oral work are therefore usually pointed out in the notes addressed to the teacher rather than in the instructions contained within the **pupils' books**. Comprehension passages and questions may be introduced orally before they are tackled in writing. Occasionally they may be purely oral. Throughout the Development Books there is a system of bulleted stimulus questions. Again, these should encourage discussion and thought and are not necessarily intended to be answered either literally or in writing.

The teaching notes also draw attention to changes in the paragraph styles found in **NE**. Original text has a fully blocked first paragraph followed by indented paragraphs, but quoted material retains its original paragraph style. This is most noticeable in the **Development** track, where extracts from traditional and modern fiction are frequently used. These variations in style provide an opportunity for encouraging children to think about the presentation of English and the reasons for these conventions of style, and to share their ideas with the group or class.

The various teaching approaches and methodologies adopted in these books will not be new to most teachers, and will ensure variety and maximise interest levels.

The comprehension has an emphasis on the literal in the **Skills** track, where it is intended above all to train the child to read the text, or to look carefully at the pictures for understanding and information. Inferential comprehension is introduced, mainly in the **Development** track, so that children can develop their ability to 'read between the lines', and form opinions about what they read. Teachers are encouraged to develop children's listening and speaking skills by trying the comprehension orally, and by asking the children to make up their own cloze and comprehension activities for each other. It is important that children read widely on subjects that are of interest to them, so individual or group research efforts using class reference books or other material should be facilitated. **NE** is planned to discourage simple copying and encourage children to read – with accuracy – the lines, between the lines and beyond the lines.

In **Skills Book** 5, the answers supplied in the Teaching Notes are, for convenience, often the missing words only, even though the questions may have required the answer in sentence form.

The vocabulary and grammar sections in **Skills Book** 5 introduce concepts in line with the curriculum documents, but also take account of teachers' expectations. The punctuation exercises and activities are gently graded and sometimes repetitive, in recognition of the need to provide regular reinforcement.

Whilst **NE** is not a comprehensive spelling programme, nevertheless it includes, through a combination of approaches, visual and aural activities to teach or reinforce the main spelling patterns, exercises covering notorious difficulties and teaching of the main rules.

As with earlier books, **Development Book 5** continues to give children a wide variety of stimulus material to analyse and use as models for their own writing. The glossary has been omitted as, by this stage, dictionary use should be encouraged. The written work is a consolidation from earlier books leading on to more varied and demanding writing tasks.

Along with a continued emphasis on purpose and audience, children are encouraged to plan, draft, revise, proof-read and present a neat, correct and clear final copy of their work. Initially, this has been done by providing a series of stages to work through, as children often find it very difficult to look critically at their own work. Asking them to check specifics such as spelling and punctuation is the first step in making them realise that their attempts can be changed, and this will eventually lead on to looking critically at style, vocabulary, etc.

Narrative writing is developed by looking at specific types of stories, e.g. adventure stories and science fiction stories. The 'plot, setting, character' basis remains constant throughout, but different types of stories rely more heavily on one or other of these elements. Children are asked to consider the intended effect on the reader when constructing their stories.

Paragraphing is introduced in the context of factual writing as paragraph divisions are easier to identify here than in narrative, imaginative or personal writing, where a more intuitive approach on the part of the individual is needed.

Occasionally reference is made to using a computer for more appropriate, professional types of layout for travel guides and magazine articles, but the authors are well aware of the organisational and time difficulties inherent in such usage and, for the most part, it is left to the discretion of the teacher.

Clearly **Skills Book 5** and **Development Book 5** are designed to allow individual and independent work, but teachers will recognise both those pupils who will from time to time benefit from more support, and where on occasion some activities might benefit from collaborative endeavour.

Nelson English Skills Book 5 — Curriculum Correlation

Nelson English and the National Curriculum (1995) England and Wales

Programme of Study / Context	1 City life	2 London in Victorian times	3 Centaurus I	4 Lilliput	5 The library puzzle	6 The watery planet	7 Jamaica Market	8 Night	9 Rainforests	10 Machines and people	11 World religions in the UK	12 The great dinosaur mystery	13 Dragons – fact or fiction?	14 Cliffs under attack	15 Lions – the cat facts
Developing compositional skills															
Wide-ranging vocabulary															
enrichment	7	12	20	24		38	45	49	55	60, 61	66, 67	72, 74	78	84	90
encouraging choices		15			30		45			61		74		87	90
Structuring grammatically/ coherently															
nouns/pronouns	7					40	46						79, 80		
verbs/tenses	7				31			50			68		80		
adjectives/adverbs	7	14			31								80		
phrases/clauses									56			73			
sentences	9											73, 74			92
paragraphs				26										85, 86	
Developing presentational skills															
Punctuation															
capital letters							45		57					85, 86	91
full stops							45		57					85, 86	91
question marks/exclamation marks							45		57					85, 86	91
commas		13					45		57		67			85, 86	91
apostrophes							45							85, 86	91
colons											67				91
direct speech		13	20				45			61					91
letters														85, 86	
Spelling															
dictionary/thesaurus				27		38						72		84	
regular patterns		14	21			41							81		
word origins								51	57	61	69	75			93
same sounds		15													
prefix/suffix	9			25, 27			47		55					86	
Developing reading skills															
wide range	4–6	10–12	16–19	22, 23	28–30	36, 37	42–44	48	52, 53	58	64, 65	70, 71	76, 77	82, 83	88, 89
understanding	5, 6	12	19	24	29, 30	37	43, 44	49	54	58, 59	66	72	78	84	90

Nelson English and the National Curriculum (1995) England and Wales

Programme of Study Context	1 City life	2 Victorian times	3 Do you believe in ghosts?	4 Other worlds	5 Advertising	6 The unsinkable *Titanic*	7 Jamaica	8 Night	9 Extinction!	10 Life in the factories	11 Moral tales	12 The mystery of the *Mary Celeste*	13 Weird and wonderful	14 Danger on the cliff!	15 Cats
Using different forms for different purposes															
Functional writing, incl. purpose/audience/planning/forms	7, 9	14, 15			30–33	37, 39	44–47		56, 57, 59	62–64		77		87–89	96
Personal writing, incl. purpose/audience/sequencing/depicting emotion/forms	9		21	27		37, 39	45	51, 53		65		77	83	89	96
Imaginative writing, incl. drafting/plot, setting, character/poetry	9	14, 15	18, 21	24, 26		37, 39	45	51, 53		65	69, 71	74, 75, 77	81, 83	87, 89	95
Developing reading skills															
wide range	4–6, 8	10–14	16–18, 20	22, 25–27	28	34, 36, 38	40–43	48, 49, 52	54, 55, 58	60, 61, 63, 64	66, 68–70	72, 73, 76	78–80, 82	84–86	90–94
understanding	6, 9	12, 15	18	23, 26	29	35, 37	44	48–50	55, 56, 59	61, 63, 64	67	73, 77	80	84–86	92, 94

Nelson English Skills Book 5 Curriculum Correlation

Nelson English and the Scottish Guidelines English Language 5 – 14

Programme of Study / Context	1 City life	2 London in Victorian times	3 Centaurus I	4 Lilliput	5 The library puzzle	6 The watery planet	7 Jamaica Market	8 Night	9 Rainforests	10 Machines and people	11 World religions in the UK	12 The great dinosaur mystery	13 Dragons – fact or fiction?	14 Cliffs under attack	15 Lions – the cat facts
Punctuation and structure															
capital letters							45		57					85, 86	91
full stops							45		57					85, 86	91
question marks/ exclamation marks							45		57					85, 86	91
commas		13					45		57		67			85, 86	91
apostrophes							45		57					85, 86	91
colons											67				91
direct speech		13	20				45			61					91
letters														85, 86	
Spelling															
graduated spelling									57			75			93
spelling rules	9	15	21	27	33	41	47	51		61	69		81	87	
dictionary/thesaurus				27		38						72		84	
Knowledge about language															
nouns/pronouns	7					40	46						79, 80		
verbs/tenses	7				31			50			68		80		
adjectives/adverbs	7	14			31								80		
phrases/clauses									56			73			
sentences	9											73, 74			92
paragraphs				26										85, 86	
Reading comprehension	5, 6	12	19	24	29, 30	37	43, 44	49	54	58, 59	66	72	78	84	90

Nelson English and the Scottish Guidelines
English Language 5–14

Programme of Study / Context	1 City life	2 Victorian times	3 Do you believe in ghosts?	4 Other worlds	5 Advertising	6 The unsinkable *Titanic*	7 Jamaica	8 Night	9 Extinction!	10 Life in the factories	11 Moral tales	12 The mystery of the *Mary Celeste*	13 Weird and wonderful	14 Danger on the cliff!	15 Cats
Functional writing, incl. purpose/audience/planning/forms	7,9	14, 15			30–33	37, 39	44–47		56, 57, 59	62–64		77		87–89	96
Personal writing, incl. purpose/audience/sequencing/depicting emotion/forms	9		21	27		37, 39	45	51, 53		65		77	83	89	96
Imaginative writing, incl. drafting/plot, setting, character/poetry	9	14, 15	18, 21	24, 26		37, 39	45	51, 53		65	69, 71	74, 75, 77	81, 83	87, 89	95
Reading comprehension (literal/inferential)	6, 9	12, 15	18	23, 26	29	35, 37	44	48–50	55, 56, 59	61, 63, 64	67	73, 77	80	84–86	92, 94

Nelson English Skills Book 5 Curriculum Correlation

Nelson English and the Northern Ireland English Curriculum Orders

Programme of Study Context	1 City life	2 London in Victorian times	3 Centaurus!	4 Lilliput	5 The library puzzle	6 The watery planet	7 Jamaica Market	8 Night	9 Rainforests	10 Machines and people	11 World religions in the UK	12 The great dinosaur mystery	13 Dragons – fact or fiction?	14 Cliffs under attack	15 Lions – the cat facts
Acquisition of vocabulary	7	12, 15	20	24	30	38	45	49	55	60, 61	66, 67	72, 74	78	84, 87	90
Grammatical conventions and Standard English															
nouns/pronouns	7				40	46						79, 80			
verbs/tenses	7			31			50			68		80			
adjectives/adverbs	7	14		31								80			
phrases/clauses									56			73			
sentences	9											73, 74			92
paragraphs			26											85, 86	
Conventions of punctuation															
capital letters						45		57						85, 86	91
full stops						45		57						85, 86	91
question marks/exclamation marks						45		57						85, 86	91
commas		13				45		57			67			85, 86	91
apostrophes						45								85, 86	91
colons											67				91
direct speech		13	20			45			61						91
letters														85, 86	
Conventions of orthography (spelling)															
common patterns	9	15	21	27	33	41	47	51		61	69		81	87	
dictionary/thesaurus				27	38							72		84	
Reading comprehension	5, 6	12	19	24	29, 30	37	43, 44	49	54	58, 59	66	72	78	84	90

Nelson English Development Book 5 Curriculum Correlation

Nelson English and the Northern Ireland English Curriculum Orders

Programme of Study Context	1 City life	2 Victorian times	3 Do you believe in ghosts?	4 Other worlds	5 Advertising	6 The unsinkable *Titanic*	7 Jamaica	8 Night	9 Extinction!	10 Life in the factories	11 Moral tales	12 The mystery of the *Mary Celeste*	13 Weird and wonderful	14 Danger on the cliff!	15 Cats
Writing for a purpose and readership	5, 7, 9	14	19, 21	26, 27	29, 31–33	37, 39	44, 46, 47	51, 53	58, 59	65	71	77	83	87–89	95, 96
Planning the writing	7, 9	15	19, 21	24	30–32	37	44–46	50, 51	56, 57, 59	62–65	69, 71	74, 75	81	85, 87–89	95, 96
Reading comprehension	6, 9	12, 15	18	23, 26	29	35, 37	44	48–50	55, 56, 59	61, 63, 64	67	73, 77	80	84–86	92, 94

Nelson English Skills Book 5

Numbers refer to pages in Skills Book 5
• see relevant Teacher's Resource Book for details.

Scope and Sequence: Grammar and Punctuation

	F	Bk1	Bk2	Bk3	Bk4	Bk5
abbreviations			•			32
addresses		•		•		85
adjectives	•	•	•	•	•	
adjectives/possessive						14
adverbs			•	•	•	
apostrophe		•	•		•	
article						14
capitals	•	•	•	•	•	45/91
clauses					•	56/73
colon						91
commas		•	•	•	•	13/45/91
comparative	•	•	•	•	•	
contractions		•	•		•	91
conjunctions	•	•		•	•	56/92
consonants	•	•				
direct speech			•	•	•	20/61/91
editing				•		
exclamation marks			•		•	91
full stops	•	•	•	•	•	91
hyphens					•	
indirect speech				•		20
inverted commas			•	•	•	20/61/91
letter writing				•	•	85
negatives					•	
nouns/abstract					•	40/79
nouns/collective	•		•	•	•	
nouns/common	•	•			•	
nouns/proper	•	•			•	
paragraphs			•	•		26
'parts of speech'						7/80
phrases		•			•	73
plural	•	•	•	•	•	
possessive nouns			•	•		
predicate			•	•		92

	F	Bk1	Bk2	Bk3	Bk4	Bk5
prepositions	•				•	
pronouns	•			•	•	56
pronouns/possessive					•	14
pronouns/relative						46
punctuation	•	•	•	•	•	13/20/26/ 32/45/61/ 67/85/91
question marks	•	•	•	•	•	91
sentences/simple	•	•	•	•		92
sentences/compound				•		92
singular	•	•	•			
spoken English					•	
subject			•	•		
superlative	•	•	•	•	•	
syllables				•		32
titles	•				•	
verbs	•	•	•			31
verbs/active: passive					•	50
verbs/agreement				•	•	
verbs/auxiliary			•	•	•	68
verbs/tense				•	•	
vowels	•	•	•			
words	•					

Nelson English Skills Book 5

Numbers refer to pages in Skills Book 5
• see relevant Teacher's Resource Book for details.

Whilst many of the spelling patterns will be introduced by teachers in the context of the work in the Foundation Level, systematic teaching of the spelling patterns begins in Skills Book 1.

Scope and Sequence: Spelling

Pattern	F	Bk1	Bk2	Bk3	Bk4	Bk5	Examples
alphabet	•	•	•	•			
initial letters	•						
short vowels	•						cat/log
ch	•		•				chip
sh	•	•	•				shop
th		•					thin
ar		•					car
ck		•					sack
oo		•					book/food
ee		•					bee
ea		•	•				sea/head
ow		•					cow/crow
ou		•					mouse
a – e		•					game
i – e		•					kite
o – e		•					rope
u – e		•					use
ing/double cons't.		•			•	33	sitting
ing/drop e		•				9	making
ear		•		•			hear
wa		•					was
making plurals		•	•	•	•	51/69	
soft c		•		•			face
er			•				letter
ir			•				bird
ur			•				nurse
o as/u/			•				mother
ai			•				nail
ay			•				play
or			•				fork
igh			•				high
ew			•				few
oy			•				toy
oi			•				boil
aw			•				fawn
oa			•				boat
silent letters			•	•	•		knife/write
ough			•				thought
ed suffix				•		33	jumped
le/el/al				•			table/travel/hospital

Pattern	F	Bk1	Bk2	Bk3	Bk4	Bk5	Examples
tch				•			catch
'i before e'				•			chief
dge endings				•			bridge
age endings				•			message
tion endings				•			station
able endings				•	•		enjoyable
ible endings				•	•		possible
ure endings				•			picture
are				•			care
ness suffix				•			darkness
ght endings				•			sight
sure endings					•		measure
augh					•		caught
ckle					•		pickle
ssion					•		confession
l or ll					•		skilful
French derivations					•		campaign
ance/ence					•		entrance/silence
gue endings					•		catalogue
ous/ious					•	21	generous/delicious
ery/ary						14	slippery/missionary
'e' ending and suffixes						9	waking/wakeful
'y' ending and suffixes						47	ugly/ugliness
adding prefixes						86	dissatisfy

Nelson English Skills Book 5

Numbers refer to pages in Skills Book 5

• see relevant Teacher's Resource Book for details.

Scope and Sequence: Vocabulary

	F	Bk1	Bk2	Bk3	Bk4	Bk5
abbreviations			•			32
acronyms						7
alliteration				•		60
alphabetical order	•	•	•	•		
anagrams					•	21
antonyms	•		•	•		87
borrowed words		•			•	
changing words						49
classifying	•	•	•			
codes		•	•	•		
collective nouns			•	•		90
comparatives	•	•	•	•	•	
compound words		•	•	•	•	
confusing words		•	•	•	•	30/31
contractions		•	•		•	
conversation words						20
days	•	•				
definitions		•	•		•	84
dialect					•	
dictionary	•	•	•		•	27/38/93
eponyms						67
foreign words					•	
gender words			•	•		12/13
glossary			•	•		
glyphs			•			
homonyms			•		•	
homophones		•		•	•	15
hyperbole					•	
hyphenated words					•	
idioms					•	60/79
interjections					•	
metaphors						38/39
months	•	•				
number words	•				•	
onomatopoeia				•	•	60
over-worked words				•	•	
palindromes				•		
plurals	•		•	•	•	
prefixes			•	•	•	25/27/55/86
proverbs					•	
puns						78
question words	•		•			
redundant words						45
repetition						60
rhyming words	•		•	•		
root words				•	•	
sign language				•		

	F	Bk1	Bk2	Bk3	Bk4	Bk5
similes			•	•		
spoonerisms					•	
suffixes			•	•	•	25/27/33/41
superlatives	•		•	•	•	
syllables				•		32
synonyms	•		•	•	•	60/66/87
thesaurus				•	•	31/72
word associations				•		
word families			•	•		
word webs						84
words within words			•	•	•	

Development Track Scope and Sequence

The units in each of the **Development Books** comprise the following:

Stimulus

The stimulus material within each book is varied to allow children to read and experience a wide range of genres including modern and traditional poetry; modern and long-established fiction; traditional tales, such as myths and legends; factual material in the form of text, charts, diagrams, etc; famous paintings and pictures.

It is left to the teacher's discretion as to how this stimulus material is introduced. It can be read, looked at and discussed by the class in groups, or children can tackle it individually.

Comprehension

Following each unit stimulus are comprehension questions. These are usually both literal – reading for understanding and information, and inferential – allowing children to engage with and respond to the stimulus. No specific writing instruction is given, to allow the teacher to use a variety of approaches – class discussion; group discussion/writing and reporting back; individual writing.

Some exercises request written sentences in response but it may sometimes be more appropriate to allow other kinds of answer to be offered, such as pictures or oral answers.

Writing

The writing tasks vary according to the aims of the unit. In some they are related in context to the stimulus material, but sometimes they are related directly to stimulus passages in terms of style, purpose and audience, so that the stimulus can be used by the children as a model for their own writing.

The writing tasks are progressive, in that each style of writing is made up of various elements. Each element is introduced in turn and children are given the opportunity to build up their competence before tackling the whole.

For example, in narrative writing, the elements of plot, timing, setting and characters are introduced in turn, allowing children to build the whole picture of what is meant by 'write a story'. There is then detailed work on story beginnings and endings, deeper characterisation, non-sequential plot, etc., to give the opportunity for more interesting and complex writing. Similarly, diaries are initially introduced as ways of keeping records, but progress from listing events to examining and recording thoughts, feelings and reactions. Also, note-taking is initially tackled through looking for and recording specific pieces of information, but it progresses to much more broadly-based research skills.

By the end of the course, children will have learnt the craft of writing in a progressive and discretely structured way. They will have an understanding of, and will have practised, story writing, imaginative writing, descriptions, writing from personal experience, discursive writing and factual writing in a range of forms.

A word about poetry writing

Poetry is used extensively as stimulus material throughout **Nelson English** but there are few occasions on which the children are asked to write a poem. The authors believe that poetry writing is too important and too difficult a skill to be lightly included in most units. The best children's poetry comes from an interaction between teacher and pupil and it is for the teacher to decide when this important kind of writing is most appropriate, and for which children. Different children will be ready for different kinds of poetry writing at different times as they progress through the material. Poetry writing can be a substitute for many of the prose writing tasks, or may be added to a unit's work, but the teacher is in the best position to decide the suitability of doing this, and to decide which children will respond postively. This is why the prescriptive poetry writing in **Nelson English** goes little beyond acrostics and limericks.

Personal choice

This section appears in each of the units in Book 5. This is to give pupils the opportunity to use the expertise they have built up in various forms of writing and can provide the basis of 'evidence' for assessing the competence of individuals. Some of the assignments can be used as timed pieces of work.

Pcm 2 in Unit 1 is a chart for the children to record their choice; this allows the teacher to ensure that a wide variety of writing is tackled. Some of the assignments lend themselves to class/group discussion, especially those concerned with looking at various shades of opinion on a given topic. This work provides the basis for discursive writing.

Nelson English Development Books

Scope and Sequence

Foundation

Writing	Examples
Comprehension	literal, inferential, picture from a variety of stimuli
Sentences	completing and writing
Narrative	picture sequencing completing stories
Imaginative	imaginative situations
Descriptive	familiar situations e.g. making a den
Personal	record keeping of events in diary form expressing preferences
Factual	simple reference books
Poetry	limericks
Lists	familiar contexts e.g. food, school

Book 1

Writing	Examples
Comprehension	literal, inferential, picture from a variety of stimuli
Sentences	completing and writing
Narrative	picture stories, completing stories
Imaginative	unfamiliar things e.g. Chinese dragons, life as a Roman soldier
Descriptive	use of adjectives purpose and audience familiar scenes e.g. houses, shops building up descriptions of objects e.g. trees matching written description with pictures describing pictures/drawings
Personal	expressing preferences e.g. where to live, favourite seasons, etc personal experience e.g. sounds at night, etc.
Factual	plans, instructions, rules analysing diagrams, maps research – simple reference books, dictionaries factual texts e.g. history
Poetry	acrostics
Letters	personal
Lists	specific pieces of information specific groups of words e.g. adjectives books/poems/stories on a given theme

Book 2

Writing	Examples
Comprehension	literal, inferential, picture from a variety of stimuli Emphasis on a) inferential – fictional texts; b) literal – reading for information – non-fiction
Sentences	completing – from given phrases e.g. time writing – based on research
Narrative	completing stories more complex picture stories – story structure planning a story – plot, time, character, setting book covers – fiction
Imaginative	sequence of events in unfamiliar situations imaginative element in narrative writing imaginary places and objects e.g. vehicles, islands involvement in given situation e.g. Wright Brothers' first flight, Robin Hood adventure
Descriptive	building up descriptions of objects matching written descriptions with pictures descriptive element in narrative writing descriptions from photographs settings e.g. island feelings in a given context e.g. William Tell descriptions based on information in stimulus passage
Personal	expressing preference e.g. food, jobs personal experience e.g. train journeys record-keeping of events in diary form
Factual	step-by-step instructions e.g. making a sandwich recording information in the form of a graph, chart, map research – reference books for information research – dictionary work to clarify meaning of stimulus passage non-fiction books – covers, contents page, index research – encyclopedias note-taking – specific pieces of information
Diaries	recording facts from stimulus passage based on pictures
Letters	personal – in context of stimulus passage
Lists	specific groups of words e.g. adverbs for a specific purpose – food/drink for a party

Book 3

Writing	Examples
Comprehension	literal, inferential, picture from a variety of more complex stimuli
Narrative	planning a story – setting, character, plot story beginnings story endings characters – actions and feelings
Imaginative	putting themselves in characters' places

Book 3 Continued

Writing	Examples
Descriptive	describing pictures e.g. 'No fire for the antelope' describing situations – storms descriptive element in story writing
Personal	personal preference e.g. modern classroom/Victorian classroom personal experience – facts and feelings e.g. first day at school autobiographies time line
Factual	instructions – analysis e.g. Fireworks Code recording information in the form of a graph, chart, map research – encyclopedias research – compiling fact file note-taking – specific topic e.g. Guy Fawkes diagrams – analysis fact and opinion factual reports from pictures e.g. weather interview newspaper reports
Letters	personal letters describing experience e.g. birthday
Lists	for description – adjectives for emotions
Poetry	acrostics
Persuasive	holiday brochures – purpose and audience for and against a given topic e.g. school uniform
Analysis	comparing/contrasting serious and comic treatment of given subject comparing/contrasting narrative/factual writing comparing/contrasting persuasive/factual writing styles of writing – purpose and audience simple/complex styles – purpose and audience
Plays	setting out playscript converting story into playscript

Book 4

Writing	Examples
Comprehension	literal, inferential, picture from a variety of stimuli Stimulus will be of a greater complexity and questions will lead pupils to analyse for purpose and audience
Sentences	beginning sentences – style use of present participles, conjunctions, etc.
Narrative	first person narratives full stories science fiction stories elements of adventure, suspense, etc.
Imaginative	imaginative element in narrative writing
Descriptive	atmospheric writing for specific response

Book 4 Continued

Writing	Examples
Personal	journals – events and responses personal experience – series of events
Factual	newspaper reports autobiography book blurbs note-taking business letters research
Persuasive	pros and cons
Structuring writing	paragraphs drafting rewriting
Analysis	purpose and audience

Book 5

Writing	Examples
Comprehension	literal, inferential, picture from a variety of stimuli Stimulus will be of a greater complexity and questions will lead pupils to analyse for purpose and audience
Narrative	characters – characterisation through dialogue/actions ghost stories mystery stories third person narrative
Imaginative	writing which is purely imaginary compared with writing about real situations which the writer has never experienced
Descriptive	more detailed description concentrating on a more mature vocabulary
Personal	personal responses/preferences to poetry and various styles of writing personal opinions
Factual	summary book reviews openings/endings for factual accounts use of non-prose devices e.g. charts, graphs for presenting information business letters advertising
Persuasive	discursive essays openings/endings
Structuring writing	headings sub-headings layout magazine articles
Analysis	purpose and audience intended reader response
Poetry	purpose and style use of poetic devices: alliteration, imagery, metaphor, etc.

Skills Book 5 **Scope and Sequence**

Unit	Stimulus	Comprehension	Vocabulary	Punctuation/ Grammar	Spelling	Quiz
1 **City life**	poems; early photographs; illustrations	cloze; literal; inferential; extension activities	acronyms	parts of speech	Tips for better spelling, 1: *e* + suffix	word order
2 **London life in Victorian times**	classic fiction; illustrations	literal; inferential	gender words	commas in sentences; possessive adjectives; articles	Tips for better spelling, 2: *ary/ery* endings	homophones
3 *Centaurus I*	play script extract; illustrations	multiple-choice; literal; inferential; extension activities	conversation words	direct and indirect speech	Tips for better spelling, 3: *our* + *ous* suffixes	anagrams
4 **Lilliput**	narrative extract; illustrations	literal; inferential; extension activities	building words	paragraphs	Tips for better spelling, 4: *ll* + prefix or suffix	dictionary guide words
5 **The library puzzle**	information text; illustrations	literal; inferential; extension activities	*either/or* and *neither/nor*	making new verbs; choosing adjectives; abbreviations	Tips for better spelling, 5: consonant doubling	word game
6 **The watery planet**	painting; fact file; information text	literal; multiple-choice; inferential	dictionary work; metaphors	abstract nouns	Tips for better spelling, 6: *able/ible* endings	vowel deletion game
7 *Jamaica Market*	narrative extract; poem; photographs	literal; inferential; extension activities	redundant words	punctuation marks; relative pronouns	Tips for better spelling, 7: *y* + suffix	word game
8 **Night**	information text; poem; diagram; photographs	literal; inferential; extension activities	words change	verbs: active and passive	Tips for better spelling, 8: making plurals	word game
9 **Rainforests – what's the fuss about?**	information text; photographs	literal; inferential; extension activities	prefixes	types of clause	"Words worth learning"	punctuation puzzle
10 **Machines and people**	poems; illustrations	extension activities	alliteration; onomatopoeia; repetition; synonyms; idioms	direct speech	Tips for better spelling, 9: *f* + *fe* plurals	common errors puzzle
11 **World religions in the UK**	information text; time line; photographs	cloze; extension activities	synonyms; eponyms	colons; using auxiliary verbs	Tips for better spelling, 10: *o* plurals	research activity
12 **The great dinosaur mystery**	aerial photograph; information text; photographs	literal; inferential; extension activities	using a thesaurus	adding words, phrases and clauses; improving sentences	"Thirty tricky words"	odd-one-out
13 **Dragons – fact or fiction?**	information text; poem; photographs	literal; inferential	puns	abstract nouns; idioms; parts of speech	Tips for better spelling, 11: *i* before *e*	word selection
14 **Cliffs under attack**	information text; photographs; diagram	literal; extension activities	definitions; word webs	personal letter; formal (business) letter	Tips for better spelling, 12: adding prefix or suffix	antonyms and synonyms
15 **Lions – the cat facts**	information text; fact file; photographs	literal; multiple-choice; extension activities	collective nouns	punctuation marks revision; types of sentence	"Another thirty tricky words"	cat and dictionary quiz

City life

1 **To introduce acronyms.**

2 **To revise the eight main parts of speech.**

3 **To practise the spelling rule for adding a suffix to words ending with *e*.**

4 **To demonstrate the impact of word order.**

Marking suggestion

Teachers may choose to paste photocopies of the unit answers on to cards and store these in a simple box, so the children can check their own answers, as appropriate.

Each card should be clearly labelled with the book title and unit number and title, to enable the children to find and use the correct unit answers easily.

Teaching notes		
Stimulus	early and modern photographs; poems	The stimulus is selected to link with the history curriculum and/or work on the local environment. Suggest the children collect early photographs and other artifacts that show the ways in which our lifestyles differ from those of 100 years ago. Also, encourage discussion on the benefits and advantages of living in their particular area. This might lead to 'formal' letter writing to appropriate authorities and organisations if suggestions are forthcoming about improvements that the children would like to see.
Comprehension	cloze; literal; inferential; extension activities	Part A, a short paragraph with cloze opportunities, each of which offers a range of possible answers. In Part B, the activities also require deductive thinking applied to the pupils' experiences.
Vocabulary	acronyms	Acronyms and abbreviations are sometimes confused by children. Whilst acronyms are essentially a form of abbreviation, they are distinguished by being able to be articulated as a *word*. This can be demonstrated with reference to *RAF*. If the letters are said *as a word* then this is an acronym; if the letters are articulated individually, which is more common now, then this is a conventional abbreviation.

Grammar	parts of speech	This unit revises and summarises the eight main 'parts of speech'.
		    Pcm 2 gives the opportunity to revise common and proper nouns; **Pcm 3** practises possessives, whilst **pcms 4, 5** and **6** give additional material on prepositions, conjunctions and interjections respectively.
		    As is described in the introductory notes, the **pcms** in this Teacher's Resource Book may be used to create a complete revision guide to the key skills, for which **pcm 1** is designed to provide a cover/contents list. The other 'parts of speech' have their related copymasters in other units. Refer to the grid on pages 12–13 if it is appropriate to make use of these alongside this unit.

Spelling	Tips for better spelling, 1	Adding a suffix to a word ending with *e*. Refer to Unit 2 **pcm 2** for additional support.
Quiz	word order	This **'Ploughman's Challenge'** activity can be used to stimulate discussion on word order, and how this can be used to good effect in writing.

See also: **p. 88, Development** notes.

Skills
Unit 1

Answers

Comprehension – Changing Times

A 1 greatly/a lot
2 much/considerably
3 get/travel
4 public transport/cars/ buses/trains
5 live
6 aeroplane/air
7 faraway/distant/foreign
8 discos/videos/the cinema/ computer games

Comprehension – Our Street

B 1 (Individual answers.)
2 (Opinions.)
3 (Individual answers.)

Vocabulary

A 1 Royal Society for the Prevention of Accidents
2 Oxford Committee for Famine Relief
3 United Nations Educational, Scientific and Cultural Organisation
4 United Nations International Children's Emergency Fund **or** United Nations Children's Fund
5 North Atlantic Treaty Organisation
6 Royal Air Force

Grammar

A 1 *tall* – adjective
policeman – noun
his – possessive adjective *pronoun*
2 *ran* – verb
quickly – adverb
he – pronoun
heard – verb
3 *small* – adjective
girls – noun
were screaming – verb
and – conjunction
toddler – noun
was crying – verb
4 *children* – noun
live – verb
in – preposition
street – noun
gathered – verb
around – adverb

5 *Ouch* – interjection
cried – verb
girl – noun
policeman – noun
lifted – verb
her – pronoun
off – preposition
road – noun
6 *She* – pronoun
was – verb
certainly – adverb
hurt – adjective *verb*
but – conjunction
badly – adverb

B (Individual answers.)

C Words that can be used as nouns or verbs:
tie; fire; rule; fly; lift.

Spelling

A 1 packaging
2 placed
3 statement
4 arguing
5 combination
6 safety
7 relation
8 basement
9 imagination
10 insurance
11 careless
12 sharing

Quiz

Possible answers include:

The weary ploughman plods his way homeward.
Weary, the ploughman plods his way homeward.
Plods the ploughman his weary way homeward.
His way homeward the weary ploughman plods.
His weary way homeward the ploughman plods.

See also: **p. 88, Development** notes. 25

Nelson ENGLISH

SKILLS BOOK 5
Unit 1 Pcm 1

NELSON ENGLISH
Personal study guide

name _____

Tips for better spelling:

1 Adding a suffix to a word ending with *e*
2 *ary* and *ery* endings
3 *our* + *ous* suffix
4 *ll* with a prefix, suffix or word added
5 Consonant doubling
6 *able* and *ible* endings
7 Adding a suffix to a word ending with *y*
8 Making plurals 1
9 Making plurals 2 (words ending in *f* and *fe*)
10 Making plurals 3 (words ending in *o*)
11 *i* before *e*
12 Adding prefixes and suffixes

Published by Thomas Nelson and Sons Ltd 1995

Common and proper nouns

> **Nouns** are 'naming' words. There are two main types of **noun** – **common nouns** and **proper nouns**.
>
> A **common noun** names any one of a group of similar things.
>   Examples: pen   dog   elephant
>
> A **proper noun** is the name of a particular person, thing or place. It always begins a with capital letter.
>   Examples: Aberdeen   Moira   English

A Write a **proper noun** which might go with each of these **common nouns**. The first is done for you.

1 country _____*Australia*_____   2 school _____

3 girl _____   4 car _____

5 city _____   6 teacher _____

7 friend _____   8 singer _____

B Write a **common noun** which is suggested by each of these **proper nouns**. The first is done for you.

1 *Gulliver's Travels* _____*book*_____   2 Wales _____

3 Jason _____   4 Bristol _____

5 Yorkshire_____   6 *HMS Belfast* _____

7 Mars _____   8 Atlantic _____

C Read these sentences and underline the **common nouns** in red and the **proper nouns** in blue.

1 Cardiff is the biggest city in Wales.

2 Our family visited France last year.

3 Josie, my sister, has curly hair and big brown eyes.

4 *Oliver Twist* is the name of a boy and the name of a book.

5 We saw the liner *Queen Elizabeth II* docking at Southampton.

Possessives

A **possessive noun** shows ownership, or possession, of the noun that follows.

We make a **possessive** of most *singular* nouns by adding **'s**.
  Examples: the boy**'s** coat   James**'s** coat

We make a **possessive** of most *plural* nouns that end in *s* by just adding an apostrophe (**'**).
  Examples: the boys**'** coats   the Smiths**'** car

We make a **possessive** of a *plural* noun that does not end in *s* by adding **'s**.
  Examples: the children**'s** coats   the women**'s** team

A   Write the **possessive** form of each of these nouns.

1 dog _____   2 squirrel _____

3 baby _____   4 men _____

5 Mr Jenkins _____   6 Colin _____

7 sisters _____   8 class _____

B   Rewrite these phrases using a **possessive**.

1 the friends of my mother _____

2 the sweets belonging to the children _____

3 the opinion of my doctor _____

4 the house of our neighbour _____

C   Fill the gap in these sentences by forming a **possessive** from the words in *italics*.

1 *teacher*   Our _____ car was hit by a lorry.

2 *teachers*   The _____ staffroom is often noisy!

3 *child*   The youngest _____ ball was lost.

4 *children*   The _____ ball was lost.

5 *thrush*   Have you heard the _____ song yet?

6 *thrushes*   I like the _____ songs.

Published by Thomas Nelson and Sons Ltd 1995   Nelson English © John Jackman and Wendy Wren 1995.

name _____ date _____

Prepositions

> A **preposition** is a word that shows the relationship of a noun or a pronoun to another word in the sentence.
>
> Example: Put the cornflakes *in* the cupboard.
>
> Here are some **prepositions** which we use frequently.
>
> | | | | | |
> |---|---|---|---|---|
> | about | above | against | among | around |
> | behind | beside | between | by | for |
> | from | in | of | off | on | over | through |
> | | to | towards | under | with | |

A Write three short sentences, each of which uses at least two **prepositions** from the box above.

1 _____

2 _____

3 _____

B Underline the **prepositions** in these sentences.

1 They put on thick, warm clothes.

2 It was essential for them to be protected against the bitter winds.

3 The control centre said that the climber was stuck between two rocks.

4 The team climbed through the mist and driving rain.

5 When they reached the woman they found her ropes jammed under a boulder.

6 They wrapped her in warm blankets and put her on a stretcher.

7 The rescuers headed back towards the road.

8 The woman climber would always be grateful for the skills of the brave Mountain Rescue volunteers.

name _____ date _____

Conjunctions

A **conjunction** is a word which is used to join words or groups of words.

   Example: Carl *and* Yuri lived in the same street.

Here are some **conjunctions** which we use frequently.

and	but	or	although	as	because
before	for	however	if	nor	since
so	than	that	though	unless	
	until	when			

A Write three short sentences, each of which uses at least two **conjunctions** from the box above.

1 _____

2 _____

3 _____

B Write a suitable **conjunction** in each of the gaps in these sentences.

1 Mum _____ Dad were in a hurry.

2 "We can't leave _____ the baby-sitter comes," said Mum.

3 "I'll look after the baby _____ you'll be late for work," I said.

4 I wasn't in a hurry _____ Joe's Dad was giving us a lift in his car today.

5 I thought I would get to school on time, _____ I was still pleased when I saw the baby-sitter arrive.

6 It was crowded in the car _____ Joe had also offered a lift to Lizzie _____ Scott.

Interjections

> An **interjection** is a word (or group of words) that expresses emotion.
>
> If the interjection expresses a strong feeling it is followed by an **exclamation mark,** and if it expresses only mild emotion it is followed by a **comma**.
>
> Examples: "Wow, I'm hungry," complained Pete.
>
> "Ouch! That hurt!" exclaimed Chris.
>
> Here are some commonly used **interjections**.
>
>

A Write sentences using these **interjections** with an *exclamation mark*.

1 Oh! _____

2 Ouch! _____

3 Help! _____

4 Sh! _____

5 Wow! _____

B Write sentences using these **interjections** with a *comma.*

1 Help, _____

2 Ah, _____

3 Whew, _____

4 Ssh, _____

5 Wow, _____

Published by Thomas Nelson and Sons Ltd 1995

London life in Victorian times

1 To revise gender words.

2 To practise using commas within sentences.

3 To introduce possessive adjectives.

4 To introduce articles.

5 To practise spellings with *ary* and *ery* endings.

6 To give further practice of significant homophones.

Teaching notes		
Stimulus	extract from *Oliver Twist*; illustrations	This short, evocative passage has proved a good stimulus for drama work. Activities might range from mime, role-play in pairs (Oliver and Sikes), through to the production of a short play (in modern idiom?), radio play or even video, the latter with particular emphasis on facial expression.
Comprehension	literal; inferential	The questions are devised to require more extended answers in section B, which will probably be more effectively handled following group discussion guided by the teacher.
Vocabulary	gender words	This unit revises work introduced earlier, extending from nouns into pronouns.
Punctuation	commas	The use of commas in lists is revised as a prelude to a pragmatic approach to the use of commas to aid meaning in sentences. **Pcm 1** provides support in practising the use of commas in lists, to improve meaning and as an essential component of the punctuation of direct speech.
Grammar	possessive adjectives; articles	In this section possessive adjectives are distinguished from possessive pronouns. Some programmes at this level do not seek to make the distinction, but if it can be grasped, it helps to underpin the understanding of both parts of speech. Articles are quickly and easily grasped, and their function as 'special' adjectives, whilst not crucial in itself, enables children to categorise these frequently-used words when considering the eight main 'parts of speech'. **Pcm 1** (in Unit 4) provides support on adjectives in general, and articles in particular, if required.
Spelling	Tips for better spelling, 2	*ary* and *ery* endings. **Pcm 3** gives additional support.
Quiz	homophone puzzle	**Pcm 4** gives opportunities to support and extend a theme, the understanding of which is important as an aid to improved spelling. The copymaster also revises homonyms.

See also: **p. 91, Development** notes.

Skills
Unit 2

Comprehension

A 1 Gas lighting was used in public houses.
2 There were so many animals in the street because it was market morning, and they were either going to be sold or pulling carts full of goods for sale.
3 Oliver and Sikes passed St Andrew's Church at close to seven o'clock.
4 They were heading towards Isleworth.
5 The cart-driver realised that Oliver was having difficulty keeping up with Sikes when he saw that Oliver was out of breath.

B 1 (Individual answers.)
2 (Opinions, such as: to resist arrest if anyone discovered that he had kidnapped Oliver; because he was going to commit a crime, especially burglary; to threaten Oliver; etc.)
3 a it was beginning to get fully light
b Gradually, other shops began to open up for the day
c the terrible/harsh/ thunderous noise/racket/roar/ clattering etc.
d pretending to be as polite as he knew how

Vocabulary

A 1 boy   2 mother
3 man   4 bride
5 her   6 wife
7 son   8 he
9 bull   10 queen
11 duck   12 Mrs/Ms

B Answers from the passage include:

Masculine	Feminine
men(N)	women(N)
countrymen(N)	
boys(N)	
he(P)	
father(N)	

Common	Neuter
they(P)	time(N)
people(N)	road(N)
labourers(N)	day(N)
donkey(N)	lamps(N)
livestock(N)	etc;
you(P)	it(P)
them(P)	

Punctuation

A 1 Countrymen, butchers, drovers, hawkers, boys, thieves, idlers and vagabonds were mingled together.
2 The whistling of drovers, the barking of dogs, the bellowing of oxen and the bleating of sheep resounded from every corner of the market.
3 The public houses, with gas lights burning inside, were already open.
4 Oliver, quickening his pace into a trot, did his best to keep up.
5 "Yes, he's my boy," replied Sikes, looking hard at Oliver.

Grammar – Possessive adjectives

A 1 his
2 their
3 Our/My
4 her
5 its
6 your

Grammar – Articles

A articles: A, the, an, a
possessive adjectives: my, our, Your, our, my, its, your, my
adjectives: small, wizened, old, last, glass, scraggy, old, five, sore, old, red.

Spelling

A 1 bakery, thundery, monastery, missionary, revolutionary, cemetery, burglary, silvery, stationery or stationary, drapery, dysentery.
2 anniversary
3 stationery/stationary (Individual answers.)

Quiz

A leek/leak
B key/quay
C hare/hair
D boy/buoy

Using commas

> We use **commas** between items in a list or between groups of words.
>> Example: From their spacecraft the astronauts could see the lights of Delhi, Calcutta, Singapore and Bangkok.
>
> (Remember to use *and* or *or* before the final item in a list, and not a comma.)

A Add commas where needed in these sentences.

1 Pete James Sammy Alice and Josie are good friends.

2 I like individual sports such as swimming cycling running and jumping more than netball rounders or hockey.

3 When writing a business letter it should be brief polite correctly set out and carefully checked for mistakes.

> We use **commas** in a sentence to help the reader know where to make a short pause.
>> Examples: The idea of playing netball, especially in hot weather, fills me with dread.
>>
>> Yes please, I'd love a cold drink.
>>
>> I know the rules, do you?

B Add commas where needed in these sentences.

1 Dr Jackson his dentist said he should clean his teeth more often.

2 No I don't think we have met before.

3 Will and I are going to Timber Lodge a summer camp by the sea.

4 James Sarah's brother has done well in his exams.

> We use **commas** to separate the actual words spoken in direct speech from the rest of the sentence.
>> Example: "What a great idea," said the man.

C Add commas where needed in these sentences.

1 "I thought you swam well today " said her brother.

2 "Thanks, but I feel exhausted now " she replied.

Published by Thomas Nelson and Sons Ltd 1995

name _____ date _____

Tips for better spelling: 1

> To add a **suffix** (word ending) when the word ends with **e**:
>
> ★ **drop** the **e** if the suffix begins with a **vowel**
> Examples: wake/waking   shame/shaming
>
> ★ **keep** the **e** if the suffix begins with a **consonant**
> Examples: wake/wakeful   shame/shameful
>
> *Some exceptions:* true/truly,   argue/argument

A   Add these suffixes to each of the words. Write the new word that is formed.

1   package + ed   _____

2   face + ing   _____

3   state + ly   _____

4   argue + ing   _____

5   quick + ly   _____

6   improve + ment   _____

7   relate + ive   _____

8   establish + ment   _____

9   imagine + ing   _____

10   insure + ed   _____

11   care + ful   _____

12   frighten + ing   _____

package

frighten

insure

quick

Spelling rules don't always work in every case – if in doubt, check in a dictionary!

Tips for better spelling: 2

Most words that end in **ary** are adjectives or 'people' nouns.
    Examples: imagin**ary**   mission**ary**

Most words that end in **ery** are nouns, but not people.
    Examples: machin**ery**   bak**ery**

Some adjectives end in **ery** because they are made from words that end in **er**.
    Examples: thund**er**   thund**ery**;   powd**er**   powd**ery**

Spelling rules don't always work in every case – if in doubt, check in a dictionary!

A   Fill in the missing *ary* or *ery* suffixes.

1 monast _____
2 powd _____
3 prim _____
4 bak _____
5 ordin _____
6 myst _____
7 necess _____
8 secret _____
9 fish _____
10 second _____

11 catt _____
12 diction _____
13 cutl _____
14 planet _____
15 butt _____
16 tann _____
17 show _____
18 batt _____
19 auxili _____
20 flatt _____

name _____ date _____

Homophones and homonyms

> **Homophones** are words that *sound the same* but are *spelt differently*.
> Example: Can you **see** the **sea**?
>
> **Homonyms** are words that *sound and are spelt the same*, but which have *different meanings*.
> Example: If you **rock** the boat we might hit that **rock**.

A   Write a **homophone** for each of these words.

1 week _____   2 grate _____   3 meet _____

4 by   _____   5 here _____   6 road _____

7 where _____   8 soul _____   9 horse _____

B   Underline the definition of the correct **homonym**.

1 The dog's *bark* frightened the intruder.   noise a dog makes   part of a tree

2 May I have a *can* of orangeade?   able to   metal container

3 Take care as you *alight* from the bus.   get down from   on fire

4 I've opened an *account* at the bank.   explain   amount of money

C   Underline the correct **homophone**.

The (to, too, two) friends walked slowly (passed, past) the old shed.

"Did (you, ewe) (here, hear) that sound?" said Toby.

"Yes, (I, eye) (heard, herd) it," replied Jason.

"The (son, sun) is (sow, so) hot it's making the roof creak," suggested Toby.

"That was (no, know) roof creak," laughed Jason, nervously.

Centaurus I

1 To encourage the use of alternatives to *said*.

2 To revise direct and indirect (reported) speech.

3 To learn the rule for adding the *ous* suffix to words ending with *our*.

4 To introduce anagrams.

Teaching notes

Stimulus	extracts from *Centaurus I*; illustrations	This short extract provides further opportunities for play reading or other drama activities. Groups might discuss how the play could be continued with each group making an audio tape, as if for a radio broadcast, of how the story ends. Encourage the use of simple sound-effects.
Comprehension	multiple-choice; literal; inferential; extension activities	Part A provides a simple multiple-choice exercise requiring literal interpretation of the passage. Part B asks for answers written in sentences, and requires both literal and deductive interpretation of the text.
Vocabulary	conversation words	The unit suggests 32 alternatives to *said*. These might be made into a chart for permanent and regular reference, with children being encouraged to add other words.
Grammar	direct and indirect speech	To extend the activity, pupils might be asked to select a short section from the passage and to write it as both direct and indirect speech.
Spelling	Tips for better spelling, 3	Adding the *ous* suffix to words ending with *our*. **Pcm 1** provides additional support, and encourages dictionary use as a support to better spelling.
Quiz	anagrams	An opportunity to learn about anagrams in the context of a simple word game.

Answers

Comprehension

A 1 2000
  2 Fermi
  3 on a tape
  4 years

B 1 PNR stands for point of no return, and it is important for the crew because after they reach it, they cannot turn back.
  2 *Centaurus I* left Earth because Earth was being destroyed by pollution and overcrowding, and the crew's ancestors had sent their children off to find a new life.
  3 Some members of the crew are concerned about the future because they may find that Centaurus Proxima cannot support life, and they would prefer to return to Earth or stay on board the ship.
  4 (Individual answers.)

Vocabulary

A (most likely answers; many others are possible)
1 warned/objected/remarked/urged/pleaded
2 retorted/objected/grumbled/muttered
3 growled/replied/grumbled/muttered/drawled
4 asked/inquired/interrupted/mumbled/whispered
5 answered/replied/explained
6 retorted/answered/objected/remarked/replied/grumbled
7 warned/yelled/shouted/sobbed/cried/exclaimed/pleaded/called
8 retorted/stammered/laughed/cried/exclaimed
9 asked/inquired/cried/interrupted/exclaimed

Grammar

A 1 Don anxiously asked what would happen if we/they ran out of fuel.
  2 The Captain replied that that simply wasn't possible.
  3 Leaping to his feet, Grant shouted that that was a ridiculous claim.
  4 Captain Fermi warned him to be very careful what he said. He said that he was in charge of the craft and he wouldn't have insubordination.

B 1 "Well, Margaret," said Michelle, "I think Grant has said too much."
  2 "Sit down, Grant," encouraged Don, holding his arm.
  3 "Time's running out, Don," muttered Grant.
  4 "Don't worry," Don reassured him, "we're safer going on than trying to return to Earth."

Spelling

A 1 rigorous
  2 laborious
  3 vigorous
  4 vaporous

Quiz

a stinging insect – wasp
where lots of trees grow – forest
an important organ in the body – heart
large, round fruit – melons
a large musical instrument – organ
where we often go on holiday – seaside

See also: **p. 93, Development** notes.

name _____   date _____

Tips for better spelling: 3

To add the suffix **ous** or **ious** to most words ending with **our**, drop the **u** in the word before the suffix is added.

Example: vapour+ous = vaporous

A Complete the words in these sentences. Use a dictionary and the word in brackets to help you.

1 He gave a very hum _____ speech.   (humour)

2 She was a most glam _____ beauty queen.   (glamour)

3 His swimming style was rather lab _____ .   (labour)

4 The plant growth was very vig _____ .   (vigour)

5 We have to be rig _____ in checking our safety equipment.   (rigour)

Lilliput

Teaching notes

Stimulus	narrative extract; illustrations	Extract from *Lilliput* (a simplified version of *Gulliver's Travels*). Having read the passage, selected children might be encouraged to read parts of *Gulliver's Travels*, or the book (or extracts) might be read aloud to the whole class by the teacher. The stimulus also provides an opportunity to enrich descriptive writing by considering the range and appropriateness of adjectives to describe scale and size, including revision of comparative and superlative forms. **Pcm 1** provides support on adjectives, including comparatives and superlatives, if required.
Comprehension	literal; inferential; extension activities	Part A is a 'true or false' activity, dependent on a literal reading of the passage, whereas Part B requires both literal and inferential interpretation of the text, with associated sentence writing to answer the questions.
Vocabulary	building words	The activities allow plurals to be considered as a form of suffix. Extend (and introduce an element of fun) by challenging pupils to find very long English words – which are bound to include suffixes and prefixes, e.g. antidisestablishmentarianism.
Punctuation	paragraphs	Teachers and schools will no doubt establish their own policy about indentation and line spaces to denote paragraphs. There is a sensible logic (and avoidance of confusion for young writers) to following the style adopted by most people using word processors, namely that no indentations are used but a line space is left between paragraphs. However, many will notice that in just about any fiction book they read, and in many non-fiction books, the traditional convention of indentation is followed, although the first line in a new chapter or section is not usually indented.
Spelling	Tips for better spelling, 4	*ll* and prefix or suffix. Words involving the addition of prefixes and/or suffixes or another word to many words where one or more parts end with *ll*. **Pcm 2** provides additional support.
Quiz	dictionary guide words	

Answers

Comprehension

A 1 Statements 1, 3, 5, 7 and 8 are true.

B 1 The tiny humans restrained Gulliver by tying him to the ground.
 2 The first words he heard spoken on Lilliput were "Hekinah degul!"
 3 (Individual answers.)
 4 (Individual answers.)

Vocabulary

A	Word	Add a prefix	Add a suffix	Add a prefix and a suffix
1	kind	unkind	kindness	unkindness
2	perfect	imperfect	perfection	imperfection
3	usual	unusual	usually	unusually
4	possible	impossible	possibly	impossibly
5	direct	indirect	directness /directly	indirectness /indirectly

B	2	thoughtfully	6	amazingly
	3	actions	7	frightening
	4	awakened	8	thankfulness
	5	peacefulness	9	powerlessness

C	1	awakened	3	frightening
	2	powerlessness	4	thankfulness

Punctuation

A (Individual answers.)

B (Individual answers.)

Spelling

A	1	spoonful	6	fateful
	2	almighty	7	shrillness
	3	fulfil	8	hillside
	4	fullness	9	careful
	5	joyful		

Quiz

industrial, industry, inedible, ineffective, inefficient, inept, inequality, inevitable, inexhaustible

See also: **p. 95, Development** notes.

Adjectives

> An **adjective** is a word that describes a noun or a pronoun.
>   Example: The man felled the *tall* tree.
>
> **Adjectives** usually tell us *what kind, how many* or *which one*.
>   Examples: *tall* tree   *four* trees   *that* tree

A   Write four **adjectives** that could be used to describe each of these nouns.

1 an aunt   _____ _____ _____ _____

2 a game   _____ _____ _____ _____

3 a friend   _____ _____ _____ _____

4 a car   _____ _____ _____ _____

5 a river   _____ _____ _____ _____

6 a baby   _____ _____ _____ _____

> **Articles** (a, an, the) are special adjectives.

B   Write **a** or **an** in front of these words, whichever is correct.

1 _____ box   2 _____ apple   3 _____ telephone   4 _____ egg

5 _____ umbrella   6 _____ ostrich   7 _____ camel   8 _____ lorry

9 When do we need to use **an** rather than **a**?

We sometimes use **adjectives** to *compare* people or things. When *two* are being compared with each other we use a **comparative** form, and when *three or more*, a **superlative** form.
(Sometimes we need to use *more* and *most*; check in a dictionary if you need help.)

C   Complete this table.

young	*younger*	*youngest*
kind		
narrow		
important		*most important*
reliable		
serious		

Tips for better spelling: 4

> To add a prefix, a suffix or another word to many words where one part or more ends with **ll**, we drop one **l** from each **ll**.
>
>   Examples: all + together = altogether;   will + full = wilful
>
> Be careful! There are several exceptions, especially words with a **ness** suffix.
>
>   Examples: smallness,   stillness,   dullness

A Join these together and put your new word in a short sentence.
Watch out for the exceptions to the rule!

1 well+come _____

2 all+mighty _____

3 un+well _____

4 full+fill _____

5 full+ness _____

6 joy+full _____

7 fate+full _____

8 shrill+ness _____

The library puzzle

1 To describe the basic organisation of libraries, with particular reference to the Dewey Decimal System.

2 To teach the correct use of *either/or* and *neither/nor*.

3 To show linkages between verbs and prepositions or adverbs.

4 To encourage greater care in the choice of appropriate words, with reference to the use of a thesaurus.

5 To revise selected abbreviations.

6 To revise certain rules relating to the addition of suffixes.

7 To revise vowels and consonants.

Teaching notes

Stimulus	information text; illustrations	A description of the organisation of the books within a school or public library.
Comprehension	literal; extension activities	The comprehension activities are split between the two main parts of the text, and are intended to assess the extent to which the principles of library organisation have been understood.
Vocabulary	using *either/or* and *neither/nor*	Stress that *neither* and *nor* are the negative forms, and as such do not interchange with *either* and *or*.
Punctuation	abbreviations	Another activity which can be extended almost indefinitely by allowing a degree of competition in seeing who can collect the most examples. The decision over the use of full stops in certain abbreviations amounts to personal choice, and opinions vary. The use of full stops in the exercises was deliberately based on the suggestions in the *spellcheck* of the authors' word processor. A useful point for discussion.
Grammar	making new verbs; choosing adjectives	Children often enjoy collecting examples of the different contexts in which selected common verbs can be used, depending on the associated preposition or adverb. Organise a competition between groups, with each group being allocated space on a board to add new examples as they are found. This activity can usefully involve parental input – and can sometimes go on for a long time! The activity concerning choosing adjectives can lead to useful group discussion about the relative merits of words and their appropriateness in different contexts. Emphasise the degree to which such decisions contain elements of subjectivity and taste.
Spelling	Tips for better spelling, 5	Key rules relating to the addition of suffixes. **Pcm 1** offers additional support. Many children find it difficult to 'hear' stress, though once understood, it can help them to remember when the letter before the suffix should be doubled.
Quiz	word game	**'Sporting Challenge'** A simple word game to revise vowels and consonants.

See also: **p. 97, Development** notes. 43

Skills
Unit 5

Answers

Comprehension – Non-fiction section

A 1 Most libraries are divided into a fiction section and a non-fiction section.
  2 Melvil Dewey invented the system for numbering non-fiction books, which is known as the Dewey Decimal System.

B 1 Buddha: 200–299
  2 wild flowers: 500–599
  3 ships: 300–399
  4 sheep farming: 600–699
  5 football: 700–799
  6 sketching: 700–799
  7 bridges: 600–699
  8 King George V: 300–399 or 900-999
  9 deserts: 900–999
 10 Shakespeare: 800–899
 11 Mozart: 700–799
 12 hospitals: 600–699

C 1 Britain's Wild Flowers: 580
  2 Our Solar System: 520
  3 Geometry for Beginners: 510
  4 Gravity and Other Forces: 530
  5 Newts and Lizards: 590
  6 Scottish Rocks and Minerals: 550

Comprehension – Fiction section

A 1 Fa–Im
  2 Aa–Ce
  3 Ch–Ez
  4 Na–Po
  5 In–Ki
  6 Aa–Ce
  7 Ti–Z
  8 Fa–Im
  9 Ti–Z

B 1 (Individual answers, but most likely to be alphabetically.)
  2 (Individual answers, perhaps suggesting that you look for a non-fiction book by the name of its author, as this is often what is most important to you.)

Vocabulary

A 1 You can read about dinosaurs <u>either</u> in this book <u>or</u> in the encyclopedia.
  2 <u>Neither</u> the school library <u>nor</u> the public library had a copy of what I needed.
  3 <u>Neither</u> James <u>nor</u> Matthew liked *The Railway Children*.
  4 I don't mind, <u>either</u> I'll read it first <u>or</u> you can read it first.
  5 It was <u>either</u> Ali <u>or</u> Manny, <u>or</u> it may even have been Danny, who borrowed the book last.

Grammar – Making new verbs

A 1–8 (Individual answers.)

B 1–5 (Use a dictionary to check on the many different possibilities.)

Grammar – Choosing adjectives

A (Individual answers.)

B Suggestions include the following:
  1 unpleasant/disgusting/awful
  2 enormous/huge/vast
  3 boggy/sodden/soggy/saturated
  4 furious/indignant/apoplectic
  5 delighted/delirious/overjoyed
  6 tempestuous/ferocious/violent

Punctuation

A 1 Dr   4 PC
  2 HM   5 ITV
  3 PM   6 MP

B 1 British Summer Time
  2 *exempli gratia* (Latin for "for example")
  3 post meridiem (Latin for "after noon")
  4 please turn over (at the foot of a page of writing)

  5 Royal Society for the Prevention of Cruelty to Animals
  6 telephone
  7 British Rail
  8 Bachelor of Science (a degree, or the person awarded it)
  9 refrigerator
 10 "I owe you"

Spelling

A 1 <u>dig</u>
  2 <u>o/mit</u>
  3 <u>hop</u>
  4 com/ic
  5 pub/lic
  6 <u>trans/mit</u>
  7 <u>it/self</u>
  8 lim/it
  9 prof/it
 10 <u>pro/pel</u>

B	add **ing**	add **ed**
ad<u>mit</u>	admitting	admitted
re<u>sist</u>	resisting	resisted
<u>target</u>	targeting	targeted
<u>benefit</u>	benefiting	benefited
sug<u>gest</u>	suggesting	suggested
dis<u>miss</u>	dismissing	dismissed
<u>borrow</u>	borrowing	borrowed

Quiz

1 cricket   2 swimming
3 football 4 rugby
5 snooker 6 hockey
7 golf   8 tennis

See also: **p. 97, Development** notes.

name _____ date _____

Tips for better spelling: 5

When adding a suffix to a short word, or one whose last syllable is stressed, look at the letter before the last letter.

If the letter before the last letter is a single vowel (a,e,i,o,u), we usually **double the last letter before adding the suffix**.

> Examples: d**i**m/dimming/dimmed
> be**gin**/beginning (last syllable is stressed)
> trans**mit**/transmitted (last syllable is stressed)

If the letter before the last letter is **not** a single vowel, we usually **just add the suffix**.

> Examples: si**ng**/singing (2nd last letter is **not** a vowel)
> re**ad**/reading (2nd last letter is **not** a **single** vowel)
> pro**fit**/profited (last syllable is **not** stressed)

This tip doesn't work for words ending with **w**, **x** or **y**.

> Examples: box/boxed/boxing;   mow/mowed/mowing

A   Complete this table. Can you spot the exception?

	*add **ing***	*add **ed***
admit	*admitting*	*admitted*
step		
drop		
greet		
pedal		
patrol		
prevail		
target		
stop		
knit		
benefit		

> Spelling rules don't always work – if in doubt, check in a dictionary!

The watery planet

Skills Book Aims:

1 **To practise and encourage dictionary use.**

2 **To introduce metaphors and revise similes.**

3 **To revise abstract nouns.**

4 **To revise *able* and *ible* endings.**

5 **To recognise that modifications occasionally occur to the base word when a suffix is added.**

Teaching notes		
Stimulus	painting; fact file; information text	The painting is Hokusai's *The Great Wave*.
Comprehension	literal; multiple-choice; inferential	Part A requires a literal understanding of the information provided; Part B is a multiple-choice activity requiring literal and inferential interpretation; Part C calls for inferential interpretations written up in sentence form.

Vocabulary	dictionary work; metaphors	Familiarity with the dictionary as an aid to better spelling is important, and the more this can be encouraged through group and class 'speed' games, and the like, the better.
		    Another idea is to get the children to create their own 'dictionary detective' challenges for each other. For example, they might pose questions which include such challenges as: find three words of more than a certain number of letters, all of which occur between two given words in their dictionary.
		    Poetry is often rich in metaphor. Make a class anthology, suitably illustrated, which focuses on metaphor in poetry.

Grammar	abstract nouns	**Pcm 1** provides extension opportunities.
Spelling	Tips for better spelling, 6	*able* and *ible* endings. **Pcm 2** provides support, and also extension activities related to the antonyms of words with these endings.
Quiz	vowel deletion game	**'Spot the Vanishing Letters'** This simple word game is provided to point out that modifications occasionally occur to the base word when a suffix is added. This usually takes the form of vowel deletion.

Answers

Comprehension

A 1 There is no water on Mars, because among the planets in our solar system, only Earth has water.
   2 Hydrogen and oxygen are the two elements which together make water.
   3 If the Earth moved closer to the sun, the water in the oceans would begin to boil.
   4 Sea water contains salt, which is not found in rainwater.

B 1 Earth
   2 Pacific
   3 10,203 metres
   4 Atlantic
   5 half the size of

C 1 For water to exist on Earth, oxygen and hydrogen must be present; and the Earth must be exactly the right distance from the sun.
   2 From the largest to the smallest, the oceans of the world are: Pacific, Atlantic, Indian, Antarctic, Arctic.
   3 Because all of Mount Everest is above sea level, we think of it as the highest mountain; much of Mauna Kea is below the sea.
   4 (Individual answers.)

Vocabulary – dictionary work

A   (Individual answers.)

B   (Individual answers.)

Vocabulary – metaphors

A 1 simile   5 metaphor
   2 simile   6 metaphor
   3 metaphor   7 metaphor
   4 simile

B 1 The sea is a hungry dog = (individual answers).
   2 That baby is a real live wire = That baby is full of life and enjoyment.
   3 She is a busy bee = She is very busy.
   4 The moon was a ghostly galleon = The moon looked like a pale ship sailing across the sky.

C   (Individual answers.)

Grammar – abstract nouns

A 2 heroism
   3 cowardice
   4 theft
   5 childhood

B 2 happiness
   3 generosity
   4 beauty
   5 stupidity
   6 activity

C 2 courageous
   3 humble
   4 wise
   5 jealous
   6 foolish

D 2 encouragement
   3 hatred/hate
   4 grief
   5 pleasure

Spelling

A 1 The sharks were invisible in the murky waters.
   2 A captain is responsible for his vessel's safety.
   3 The storm did a negligible amount of damage.
   4 Do you think it advisable to sail today?
   5 The engine was unreliable.

Quiz

1 e (wintry)
2 u (generosity)
3 e (disastrous)
4 i (exclamation)
5 u (humorous)
6 u (curiosity)
7 e (monstrous)
8 e (tigress)
9 e (carpentry)

See also: **p. 99, Development** notes.

name _____ date _____

Abstract nouns

> **Abstract nouns** deal with qualities, feelings, times or actions which you can't see, touch, taste, smell or hear.
> Example: A *magician* can be seen on the stage, but his *magic* can only be talked or thought about.

A Fill in the gaps in these sentences with an **abstract noun** that is related to the noun in *italics*.

The first is done to help you.

1 The *walker* enjoyed _____*walking*_____ .

2 My *friend* says he values our _____ .

3 The *thief* was arrested for the _____ .

> **Abstract nouns** can also be made from adjectives.
> Example: The *excellent* student received her certificate of *excellence*.
> adjective   abstract noun

B Next to each of these adjectives write the **abstract noun** that can be made from it.

1 skilful ___*skill*___   2 famous _____   3 truthful _____

4 determined _____   5 attractive _____   6 beautiful _____

> **Abstract nouns** can also be made from verbs.
> Example: To *free* a trapped dolphin is to give it *freedom*.
> verb   abstract noun

C Complete these statements with an **abstract noun**.
The first is done to help you.

1 The prisoner was pleased to be *free* when he got his ___*freedom*___ .

2 If we *speak* to someone we use _____ .

3 The cat was frightened by the noise of the _____ as we *laughed* at Dad's joke.

4 To *exaggerate* is to use _____ .

Tips for better spelling: 6

Many words have the suffix **able** or **ible**.

There is no easy way to remember when to use **able** or when to use **ible**.

However, because about five times as many words end in **able** as end in **ible**, you're safer using **able** if you're not sure which is right!

This tip will help, too.

If the *antonym* (opposite) of the word starts with **un** it is probable that it is an **able** word.

If the *antonym* (opposite) of the word starts with **il**, **im**, **in** or **ir**, it is probably an **ible** word.

Examples: ***un*eat*able***   ***ir*resist*ible***

A   Antonyms of all of these words can be made by adding one of these prefixes:

un   *im*   *in*   *ir*

Put the words in the correct boxes and add the missing letter – but be careful. There are some which disobey the rule!

vis_ble	respons_ble	advis_ble	reli_ble
approach_ble	excit_ble	poss_ble	cap_ble
prob_ble	comfort_ble	enjoy_ble	avail_ble

Antonym starts with **un**	Antonym starts with **il im in ir**

Spelling rules don't always work in every case – if in doubt, check in a dictionary!

Published by Thomas Nelson and Sons Ltd 1995

Jamaica Market

1 To suggest the desirability of avoiding the over-use of adjectives.

2 To revise all the main sentence punctuation marks.

3 To introduce relative pronouns.

4 To revise certain rules for the addition of suffixes.

Teaching notes

Stimulus	narrative extract; poem; photographs	Stimulus items include the poem *Jamaica Market*, and an extract from *Anansi the Spider Man*. The unit focuses on aspects of life in Jamaica. The opportunities for development are considerable, especially through inviting visitors, including parents, into the class to share their experiences of Caribbean life and culture. Start an anthology of stories and poetry from the West Indian tradition, and possibly from other ethnic groups.
Comprehension	literal; inferential; extension activities	As well as being presented for the pleasure of reading it in its own right, the poem is used as a vehicle to revise words which can stand as more than one part of speech. Part B seeks essentially literal answers in sentences to questions on the *Anansi* passage.
Vocabulary	redundant words	This is a simple introduction to *tautology* (Greek: 'saying the same thing twice') and *pleonasm* (Greek: 'more than enough'). Encourage the children to look out for examples, and extend to consider 'absolutes' which don't require reinforcement (for example, 'very *unique*').
Punctuation	capital letters; commas; conversations	Two exercises revise and consolidate much of the earlier work on punctuation. **Pcm 1** provides additional support on the variety of uses for capital letters, and **pcm 2** revises punctuation for ending sentences (full stop, question mark, exclamation mark).
Grammar	relative pronouns	This section considers the function of relative pronouns and when to use which relative pronouns. **Pcm 3** offers support for this as well as general revision of pronouns and particular activities to revise possessive pronouns.
Spelling	Tips for better spelling, 7	Adding a suffix to a word that ends with *y*. **Pcm 4** provides opportunities for additional support if needed.
Quiz	word game	Two word games to stimulate and amuse.

See also: **p. 101, Development** notes. 49

Skills
Unit 7

Answers

Comprehension – Anansi

A 1 Anansi and Kling Kling were no longer friends because Kling Kling had not paid his fine.
  2 Anansi tried to catch the bird by setting traps in the grass and by hiding nooses where Kling Kling liked to walk.
  3 Anansi offered Tiger a whole cow if he could catch Kling Kling.
  4 Kling Kling tricked Tiger into laughing loudly, and then he knew that Tiger was not dead and it was all a trick.

Comprehension – Jamaica Market

A 1 a pagan fruit = exciting, colourful fruit from exotic countries
    b pallid leeks = pale-coloured leeks
    c babel = great noise of people all talking at once
  2 (Individual answers.)

Vocabulary

A 1 Kling Kling was too brainy to get caught.
  2 The lady in the market was pretty though(/but) poor, so she couldn't afford expensive clothes.
  3 The huge crowd thought it was comical that Tiger should have fallen for such a simple trick.

Punctuation

A Jamaica, an island in the West Indies, is the third-largest island in the Caribbean Sea. Located south of Cuba and west of Hispaniola, Jamaica is about 146 miles (235 km) long by 51 miles (82 km) at its widest point, and has highlands running from east to west that cover a large proportion of the island. The highest part of Jamaica is in the Blue Mountains to the east. Sugar, tropical fruits, coffee and cacao are grown in quantity for sale both in Jamaica and to other countries.

B "Did you know that Christopher Columbus reached Jamaica in May 1494?" asked the teacher.
  "Yes, I did," said the boy. "My father was telling me about Jamaica's history the other day."
  "What else did he tell you, then?" enquired the teacher.
  "He told me that at that time the island was populated by Arawak Indians," replied the boy, "but these peoples soon died out and slaves were brought from Africa to work in the sugar-cane fields."

Grammar

A 1 This is the picture which I want you to give to my grandparents.
  2 Tell them it is from their grandson who wishes he was coming on the aeroplane.
  3 Please thank them for the present which they sent for my birthday.
  4 In which car are you going to the airport?
  5 It's a long flight, so don't sit next to anyone who snores!

B 1 I wanted to go with Dad, who was going to visit his parents.
  2 He took a large box of chocolates, which was a present for my grandparents.
  3 My grandparents liked the chocolates, which they ate straight away.
  4 They took Dad to their home, which is in Kingston.
  5 He was pleased to see the garden that he used to play in when he was a boy.

Spelling

A Combinations which can be made for use in sentences are:
  1 merriment, merrily
  2 haughtiness, haughtily
  3 heaviness, heavily
  4 funnily
  5 naughtiness, naughtily
  6 silliness
  7 prettiness, prettily
  8 nastiness, nastily

Quiz

STARTLING – starting, staring, string, sting, sing, sin, in, I

THEREIN – there, in, here, herein, rein, the, her, he, ere

See also: **p. 101, Development** notes.

Using capital letters

Capital letters are used to begin sentences, for the word 'I' and for the types of word listed in the table.

A Complete this table, adding another example in each row.

Titles, initials and names of people or things	*Ms S Lindsay*
Buildings	*Westminster Abbey*
Places	*Jamaica*
Names of ships and aircraft	*Concorde*
Adjectives made from names	*Welsh*
Streets	*Oxford Street*
Days and months	*Tuesday*
First and important words in titles	*The Wind in the Willows*
Names of companies	*Digital*

B Put a neat circle around the letters that should be capitals.

1 ms wanda farr, travel editor, columbus books ltd

2 nelson mandela, south africa, cape town

3 statue of liberty, city, new york, kennedy airport

4 monday, february, i, we

5 the lion, the witch and the wardrobe, book, c s lewis

6 british airways   jet   gatwick   captain jones

7 it was a rainy tuesday afternoon in december. in normal circumstances andy and i would have been feeling fed up, but not this tuesday. after school andy's mum, mrs purewal, was taking us into birmingham to see the pantomime dick whittington.

Ending sentences

There are three punctuation marks which can be used to end a sentence – **a full stop (.)**
        a question mark (?)
        an exclamation mark (!)

A   Add the correct punctuation mark at the end of each of these sentences.

1 Will you help me move to my new office

2 We thought that would be fun

3 Can we have a day off school

4 No you most certainly cannot

5 Why not

6 I'm moving on a Saturday

7 Look out

8 Ouch, that hurt

9 You must be very careful when lifting furniture

10 Thanks for all your help

B   Add the correct punctuation marks where needed in this short passage.

London is the capital city of Great Britain   It is one of the largest cities in the world   Do you know which city in the world has the biggest population

Every year thousands of people visit London   Have you ever been there   Visitors travel from all over Britain and from other parts of the world   What do you think is the most popular attraction   It's the Tower of London

Published by Thomas Nelson and Sons Ltd 1995

Pronouns

> **Pronouns** are used in place of nouns.
> Examples:
> **I me you she
> he her him it
> we us them
> they**

A Underline the **pronouns** in these sentences.

1 We have a new teacher starting next week.

2 He seems fun; I think I will like him.

3 It will be different having a man teacher.

4 They said they were sorry Mrs Walsh would not be teaching them for a while.

> **Possessive pronouns** show who or what owns something.
> Examples:
> **mine yours his
> hers ours
> theirs**

B Underline all the **pronouns** in these sentences, and put a neat circle round the **possessive pronouns**.

1 The books are his.   2 He thought it was mine.

3 Are they yours?   4 The computer is ours.

Relative pronouns are special because they do two jobs.
1 They take the place of nouns.
2 They act as conjunctions, and are **related** to the noun that is before them in a sentence.

> Example: Dad caught the aeroplane.
> The aeroplane was flying to Kingston.
>
> Dad caught the aeroplane **which** was flying to Kingston.

C Rewrite these pairs of sentences, using a **relative** pronoun (**who/whom/whose/which/that**) as a **conjunction** to join them.

1 I said I would stay and help Mum.
Mum was cleaning the car.

_____

_____

2 She cut her finger on a piece of metal.
The piece of metal had a rough edge.

_____

_____

name _____ date _____

Tips for better spelling: 7

When we add a suffix to a word that ends in **y**, sometimes we just add the suffix, **but** sometimes we change the **y** to an **i** before we add the suffix.

     Examples: enjo**y** enjo**y**ing ;   ugl**y** ugl**i**ness

Here is a tip to help you.

If the letter before the **y** is a **consonant**, change the **y** to **i** and add the suffix – *except* when the suffix is *ing*.

     Example: tid**y** tid**i**est tid**i**ly *but* tid**y**ing

If the letter before the **y** is a **vowel**, keep the **y** when adding the suffix.

     Example: pla**y** pla**y**er pla**y**ed pla**y**ing

A   Fill in the blank spaces in this table.

base word	+ ed	+ ing	+ ness	+ ly	+ ment
display			◆	◆	◆
silly	◆	◆		◆	
enjoy			◆		◆
delay			◆	◆	◆
try			◆	◆	◆
merry	◆	◆			
heavy	◆	◆			◆
study			◆	◆	◆
employ			◆	◆	
deploy			◆	◆	
pretty	◆	◆			◆
stray			◆	◆	◆

Spelling rules don't always work in every case – if in doubt, check in a dictionary!

Night

Teaching notes

Stimulus	information text; poem; illustrations	The stimulus poem is called *I Stood and Stared*. The enormity of space rarely fails to capture young people's imaginations, so this unit may lead in many different directions in terms of both content and language work. Children might be encouraged to empathise with the poet, which might lead to some short (possibly poetic) pieces of very personal writing relating to an aspect of night/space. Some children might attempt to research and create a model (suspended from the ceiling) or large, scale diagram of our solar system.
Comprehension	literal; inferential; extension activities	The questions in Part A require single sentence responses based on a literal interpretation of the text, whereas in Part B, both literal and inferential responses are required.
Vocabulary	words change	This section is intended to demonstrate, albeit briefly, that language is merely a convention which evolves and changes with time. Our understanding that certain sounds in spoken language represent particular objects, actions, feelings, etc. is simply something that a certain population in a particular place at a particular time has come to accept. Others, in other countries or in other periods of history, have made use of different sounds to express the same things. In pairs or small groups, some children might create their own simple language of nouns, verbs and possibly adjectives.
Grammar	verbs: active and passive	This topic can cause problems which careful discussion might overcome. However, for those for whom this is too challenging a concept at this point, alternative revision work on basic verb tenses is offered in **pcm 1**.
Spelling	Tips for better spelling, 8	Basic plural noun spellings. **Pcm 2** provides additional support covering *s*, *es* and *ies* plurals.
Quiz	word game	**'Lost planets'** is a simple word game relating to our solar system's planets and constellations.

Answers

Comprehension

A 1 The sun's light takes $8\frac{1}{2}$ minutes to reach Earth.

2 The universe is larger than our solar system or our galaxy.

3 The Milky Way is a galaxy, or enormous group of stars, which measures about 100,000 light years from side to side.

4 The Earth is a planet. Stars are glowing balls of extremely hot gases.

B (Individual answers.)

Vocabulary

A 2 seldom   4 bucket
  3 bitter   5 fret

Grammar

A 2 Jupiter was hit by huge meteorites in June 1994.

3 The eclipse of the sun was photographed by the scientists.

4 We were told about the Milky Way by the 'Night Sky' television programme.

B 1 The stars blinded my eyes.

2 The vastness of the universe fascinated the girls.

3 The Earth eclipsed the moon.

4 The sheer beauty of the Earth amazed the astronauts.

Spelling

A 1 poets   11 valleys
  2 stars   12 quays
  3 rushes   13 companies
  4 activities 14 grasses
  5 curries   15 torches
  6 alleys   16 ceremonies
  7 ponies   17 sounds
  8 satellites 18 fathers
  9 difficulties 19 moons
  10 boxes   20 countries

Quiz

1 Mercury/galaxy
2 Jupiter/hydrogen
3 Neptune/Celsius
4 Uranus/universe
5 Saturn/nuclear
6 Venus/satellites

See also: **p. 104, Development** notes.

name _____   date _____

Verb tenses

> The **tense** of a verb tells us when the action happens.
>
> Examples:
> Mark *plays* for the school team at present.   (**present tense**)
> Mark *played* for the school team last week.   (**past tense**)
> Mark *will play* for the school team next week. (**future tense**)

A Underline the verb or verbs in these sentences and say whether
each is in the **present, past** or **future tense**.

1 Mum is watching the match.   _____

2 Once she shouted so much she lost her voice.   _____

3 Dad will come to the next game.   _____

4 Mark plays for the school team.   _____

5 He scored a goal last week.   _____

6 He hopes he will score another next week.   _____

B Rewrite these sentences, which are in the **present tense**,
changing them to the **past tense** and the **future tense**.

1 Caroline dances in the school concert.

  past   _____

  future _____

2 All the family watch her.

  past   _____

  future _____

3 Even Granma has come.

  past   _____

  future _____

4 It is Caroline's last school performance.

  past   _____

  future _____

name _____   date _____

Tips for better spelling: 8

To make a noun **plural** we normally **add** s.
   Examples: star/star**s**   night/night**s**

But if the noun ends with **s**, **x**, **ch** or **sh** we add **es**.
   Examples: bus/bus**es**   fox/fox**es**
                  chur**ch**/chur**ches**   bu**sh**/bu**shes**

If a noun ends in **y**, we change **y** to **i** and add **es**.
   Example: story/stor**ies**

But if the letter before the **y** is a *vowel*, simply **add** s.
   Examples: da**y**/day**s**

A   Draw a line under the correct **plural** form of these words.

1 sound	sounds	soundes	soundies
2 family	familys	familyes	families
3 poet	poets	poetes	poeties
4 pony	ponys	ponyes	ponies
5 quay	quays	quayes	quaies
6 bush	bushs	bushes	bushies
7 turkey	turkeys	turkeyes	turkeies
8 fox	foxs	foxes	foxies

Spelling rules don't always work in every case – if in doubt, check in a dictionary!

B   Write the **plural** of each of these words.

1 dog _____   2 jockey _____

3 gas _____   4 activity _____

5 lorry _____   6 splash _____

7 house _____   8 fly _____

9 box _____   10 monkey_____

Rainforests – what's the fuss about?

1 To revise the most common prefixes.

2 To revise clauses, especially adjective and adverb clauses.

3 To revise selected 'tricky' spellings.

4 To practise basic sentence punctuation.

Teaching notes

Stimulus	information text; illustrations	This is one of the key 'environmental' issues and as such is not only a subject which needs to be factually researched, but also one which can and should be the basis for discussion and debate on the central issues. This can be organised within groups or individually, and might lead on to other environmental concerns.
Comprehension	literal; inferential; extension activities	Part A is a true/false comprehension activity based on a literal interpretation of the text. Part B requires empathy and deductive thought to write brief paragraphs.
Vocabulary	prefixes	**Pcm 1** gives additional support on prefixes, and **pcm 2** extends similar activities to suffixes.
Grammar	adjective and adverb clauses	This unit focuses on clauses. For those pupils who find this too challenging at this point, **pcm 3** provides an optional activity on simple subject/predicate identification. Work on clauses will be extended in Unit 12.
Spelling	"Words worth learning"	The 'tricky' words selected typify several of the types of word that cause problems at this stage. They are all well worth learning, and it can be useful to discuss in groups what are the most likely errors to be made with each of these words.
Quiz	punctuation puzzle	**'What's missing'** is a simple punctuation exercise that has been made more challenging by the omission of the word spaces.

Answers

Comprehension

A 1 false
  2 true
  3 false
  4 true
  5 true
  6 false

B (Individual answers.)

Vocabulary

A (Individual answers.)

Grammar

A 1 Life can be difficult for poor people (main)
    who live in the rainforests. (subordinate)

  2 Companies can build factories and create jobs (main)
    so that fewer people have to use the rainforests. (subordinate)

  3 It is important (main)
    that we solve this problem (subordinate)
    before all the jungles are destroyed. (subordinate)

B (Individual answers.)

Spelling

A 1 atmosphere; destroy; diseases; environment; essential; generation; government; irreplaceable; medicine; pollute; resources; scientist; sufficient; survive; torrential

  2 Many possible answers, among which are:
    sufficient – enough, plenty (S); insufficient, inadequate (A)
    essential – necessary, vital (S); inessential, unnecessary (A)
    survive – live, exist (S); die, perish (A)
    destroy – ruin (S); create, produce (A)
    irreplaceable – unique (S); common, plentiful (A)
    torrential – pouring, heavy (S); slight, light (A)
    pollute – contaminate, dirty (S); clean, purify (A)

Quiz

Britain's natural forests are now protected and are being extended. Large areas in upland regions have been planted with conifer trees to help meet our timber needs. Many people argue that these are unnatural and spoil the landscape. What do you think?

See also: **p. 106, Development** notes.

Prefixes

A **prefix** is added at the beginning of a word and changes the word's meaning.

Example: *im* (meaning 'not') + *possible* = impossible

Some prefixes have one meaning; others have several meanings. Sometimes different prefixes have the same meaning.

Examples:	prefix	meaning
	un in im non-	not
	dis in non-	lack of; opposite of
	trans	across; beyond
	mis	wrong
	anti-	against
	ex	out; former; without; from; beyond

A   Write a new word using one of the prefixes from the box. Give the meaning of each new word.

new word   *means*

1 please   _____   _____

2 just   _____   _____

3 smoking   _____   _____

4 aircraft   _____   _____

5 Atlantic   _____   _____

6 understanding _____   _____

B   Underline each prefix, and write the meaning of each word that has a prefix. Use a dictionary to help you.

1 nonstop train   _____

2 disagreeable old man   _____

3 antibiotic medicine   _____

4 international competition _____

5 irrelevant story   _____

6 predetermine the result _____

Published by Thomas Nelson and Sons Ltd 1995

name _____ date _____

Suffixes

> A **suffix** is added at the end of a word and changes the word's meaning.
>
> > Example: *ful* (meaning 'full of') + beauty = beautiful
>
> Notice how **suffixes** sometimes change the spelling of the word they are added to.
>
> Some suffixes have one meaning; others have several meanings.
>
> > Examples: suffix   meaning
> >
> > | | |
> > |---|---|
> > | *able* | able to; inclined to |
> > | *less* | without |
> > | *ous* | full of; having; containing |
> > | *y* | full of; having |
> > | *ful* | full of; as much as will fill |
> > | *al* | like; relating to; of; belonging to |

A Write a new word using one of the suffixes from the box. Give the meaning of each new word. Don't use any suffix more than once.

         new word   *means*

1 deceit   _____   _____

2 rain   _____   _____

3 mountain   _____   _____

4 enjoy   _____   _____

5 thought   _____   _____

6 nation   _____   _____

B Underline each suffix, and write the meaning of each word that has a suffix.

1 inflatable dinghy   _____

2 tearful farewell   _____

3 hazardous journey   _____

4 useless information _____

5 disposable nappies _____

6 snowy weather   _____

name _____   date _____

Subject and predicate

A simple sentence has two parts.
The **subject** is the thing or person written about.
The **predicate** is the rest of the sentence. It includes the *verb*, and tells us what is happening.

Example: The lightning / struck the chimney.

subject   predicate

A Finish these sentences by adding a **predicate** to each **subject**.

1 The fire brigade _____ .

2 Dad's old car _____ .

3 Three elephants _____ .

4 The television programme _____ .

5 My chicken _____ .

B Draw a line between the **subject** and the **predicate** in each of these sentences. Neatly underline the subject. The first has been done for you.

1 <u>Our teacher</u> / was upset that we had made such a mess.

2 We promised to clean it up.

3 Paint was everywhere.

4 The newspapers had become stuck to the floor.

5 The cleaner was cross too.

6 I doubt we'll be allowed to paint again for a while!

C Add a **subject** to complete these sentences.

1 _____ is the capital of France.

2 _____ are the largest mammals ever to have lived.

3 _____ is delighted with her new personal computer.

4 _____ hope to win tomorrow.

Published by Thomas Nelson and Sons Ltd 1995

Machines and people

Skills Book Aims:

1 To revise selected literary devices.

2 To practise direct speech punctuation.

3 To revise the spelling of plural nouns that end with *f* or *fe*.

4 To practise some common grammatical points which often cause difficulty.

Teaching notes

Stimulus	poems; illustrations	*Don't* by Michael Rosen and *The Computer's First Christmas Card* by Edwin Morgan. 　　Poems about things mechanical abound, although naturally there are still few about computers. Such poems and prose extracts can form a strong basis for a topic on local industry and technology, which often proves an ideal reason to invite parents and others to share their work experiences. It can also be a meaningful and fruitful opportunity for letter-writing by groups to local companies – collecting information or even enquiring about setting up short visits.
Comprehension	extension activities	This is intended as much to provide stimulus and starting points for discussion as to be a conventional comprehension activity.
Vocabulary	alliteration; onomatopoeia; repetition; synonyms; idioms	Ask the children, probably in pairs or small groups, to search through a selection of poetry anthologies to find further examples of each of these devices.
Punctuation	direct speech	In **pcm 1**, part A offers a simple support exercise without the complication of line breaks, and part B has additional practice including the need to start a new line for each change of speaker.
Spelling	Tips for better spelling, 9	Plural nouns that end with *f* or *fe*. 　　**Pcm 2** offers an additional support activity.
Quiz	common errors puzzle	The quiz 'Get It Right' practises selected grammatical points which frequently cause difficulty. It can be supplemented with oral activities in which the teacher asks the class to spot the deliberate mistake in a sentence.

Answers

Comprehension

A 1 toffee/coffee; gravy/baby; beer/ear; toes/nose; confetti/spaghetti; peas/knees; ants/pants; mustard/custard; jelly/telly

2 a jolly, merry, holly, berry, happy

　　b heppy, hoppy, Jarry, boppy, jorry, moppy, joppy, Chris, annery

B (Individual answers.)

Vocabulary

A 1 Any two lines would be a correct answer.

2 (Individual answers.)

B (Individual answers.)

C (Individual answers.)

D (Individual answers.)

E 1 My head was aching terribly/was too full of information, etc.

2 Together/between us, let's try to think of a plan/ solution, etc.

3 He was found in the act of committing a crime/doing something wrong, etc.

Punctuation

A 　"Hi, Jane!" shouted Bob. "That's quite some machine you're driving there."
　　"She certainly is a real beauty, and strong too," Jane replied, "but really easy to handle. All the controls are power-assisted. In fact, it's more like flying a plane than driving an earth-mover."
　　"Can I have a go?" he asked.
　　"Sorry, old mate, it's more than my job's worth to let anyone near her," Jane shouted, secretly pleased that she alone had been trusted to drive the new machine.

Spelling

A 1 thieves

2 calves

3 leaves

4 knives

5 handkerchiefs

6 wolves

7 scarves

8 loaves

9 chiefs

10 halves

Quiz

1 The bulldozer and the digger <u>were</u> both working flat out.

2 Mine is the <u>better</u> of the two computers.

3 Dad said he'd take Wes and <u>me</u> in his new lorry.

4 We <u>were</u> both very excited.

5 <u>Who's</u> left the printer on?

6 May I <u>borrow</u> your tools please?

See also: **p. 107, Development** notes.

name _____ date _____

Direct speech

We use **inverted commas** ("speech marks") to show the exact
words of a speaker, and a **comma** or another punctuation mark to
separate these spoken words from the rest of the sentence.

Sometimes the spoken words come at the beginning of the
sentence, sometimes at the end, and sometimes they are divided.

Example: Richard asked, "May I borrow your book
about chess?"

"Yes, I'll bring it tomorrow," replied Matthew.

"Thanks," said Richard, "I'll take good care of it."

A Add **inverted commas**, **commas** and other missing punctuation
marks to these sentences.

1 My Mum likes playing chess said Brian

2 So does mine said Ali

3 How good is your Mum asked Brian

4 Quite good replied Ali but I manage to beat her sometimes

5 If I came to your house said Brian would she give me a game

6 Yes, I'm sure she would said Ali with a smile

7 Why are you smiling asked his friend

8 No reason really replied Ali but I hope you don't mind being
beaten

When writing **direct speech** we start a new line when a different
person begins to speak.

B Rewrite this passage on a sheet of paper, adding **inverted
commas, commas** and other missing punctuation marks, and
begin a new line each time a different person starts to speak.

It would be excellent if we could start a chess club at school
suggested Tania. I agree said Ali. Let's ask Mr Scott if he would
mind suggested Brian. If he agrees said Tania where will we get
the money to buy the chess sets? We could have a membership
fee proposed Ali. If people wanted to join the club I don't think
they would mind paying a small amount to get us started.

Published by Thomas Nelson and Sons Ltd 1995

name _____ date _____

Tips for better spelling: 9

To make **plural** forms of nouns that end in **f** or **fe** we usually change the **f** or **fe** to **v**, and add **es**.

   Examples: wol**f**, wol**ves** wi**fe**, wi**ves**

Beware! There are several important exceptions.

A Write the **plural** of each of these words. Be careful, some don't follow the normal rule.

1 loaf _____ 2 thief _____

3 wife _____ 4 wolf _____

5 chief _____ 6 roof _____

7 half _____ 8 scarf _____

9 life _____ 10 knife _____

Skills
Unit 11

**Skills Book
Aims:**

1 To revise and use synonyms.

2 To recognise eponyms.

3 To introduce the use of colons.

4 To describe the use of auxiliary verbs in the context of verb tenses.

5 To revise the plural form of nouns that end with *o*.

World religions in the UK

Teaching notes		
Stimulus	information text; time line; photographs	The information text provides a brief summary of the main religions represented in the UK. In ethnically/religiously mixed classes it can be interesting for children to research a religious group other than their own, with a view to staging a simple exhibition. Where this is not practicable, then divide the class into groups, each of which is charged with making a detailed presentation about a different religious faith. Teachers will recognise the amount of support and direction required, but the more that each group can plan and research their material, the better.
Comprehension	cloze; extension activities	Part A requires mainly literal responses to the information provided, and Part B suggests extension activities which need careful thought.
Vocabulary	synonyms; eponyms	Synonyms have been practised throughout the course, and this is continued here, suggesting how their use can enhance the quality of written work. A part of the activity requires access to a thesaurus. **Pcm 1** provides opportunities for support and extension. Whilst eponyms are not highly significant, knowledge of them informs and often intrigues children.
Punctuation	colons	Care needs to be taken to ensure young writers don't get carried away and start using colons too liberally. Insist that they are only used for specific lists, where a full stop might otherwise have seemed the appropriate punctuation mark.
Grammar	auxiliary verbs	**Pcm 2** provides support by revising the basic verb function before introducing the auxiliary verb in its 'helper' role.
Spelling	Tips for better spelling, 10	Plural form of nouns that end with *o*. **Pcm 3** provides additional support and the opportunity for further practice.
Quiz	research activity	This is a structured activity requiring library research into religion.

See also: **p. 109, Development** notes. 65

Skills
Unit 11

Answers

Comprehension

A 1 The five largest religious groups in Britain are Christians, Muslims, Sikhs, Hindus and Jews.

2 Humanists have no specific religious beliefs but believe they have responsibilities to their fellow humans and to the planet.

3 Agnostics are people who cannot decide whether or not there is a God.

4 Those who are sure that there is no God are called atheists.

5 Jesus was born (around 500 years) after Buddha.

B (Individual answers.)

Vocabulary – synonyms

A 1 belief: religion, faith, creed, doctrine, etc.

2 major: important, great, large, significant, etc.

3 old: aged, elderly, ancient, advanced in years, etc.

4 environment: surroundings, atmosphere, place where you live, etc.

5 impossible: hopeless, unrealistic, impractical, not achievable, etc.

6 god: supreme being, divinity, deity, etc.

7 group: collection, fellowship, gathering, crowd, etc.

8 important: essential, prominent, senior, powerful, well-known, etc.

B (Individual answers.)

Vocabulary – eponyms

(Individual answers.)

Punctuation

A 1 There are important religious festivals on the following dates: January 6th, February 12th, April 3rd, May 16th and June 10th.

2 The following have been selected to sing solos next week: Ben, William, Claire, Annie, Sunil and Roy.

3 I have chosen these hymns: 15, 243, 78, 46 and 55.

Grammar

A 1 I rang the church bell this morning.

2 I had not rung it for the last three months.

3 The service began at 9.30 a.m.

4 It had begun before I had finished ringing!

5 The verger came in and took the bell-rope from me.

6 If I had taken my watch I wouldn't have made the mistake.

7 I ran home feeling very upset.

8 I felt better after I had drunk a cup of tea and eaten a biscuit.

9 The vicar came to our house and told me not to worry.

B (Individual answers.)

Spelling

A 1 sopranos
2 heroes
3 volcanoes or volcanos
4 potatoes
5 photos
6 mottoes or mottos
7 cuckoos
8 pianos
9 radios
10 cockatoos
11 cellos
12 echoes

Quiz

(Individual answers.)

See also: **p. 109, Development** notes.

name _____ date _____

Antonyms and synonyms

An **antonym** has the *opposite* meaning to another word.
 Example: poor – rich

A **synonym** has a *similar* meaning to another word.
 Example: error – mistake

A Write an **antonym** for each of these words.

1 hot _____ 2 thin _____ 3 useful _____

4 narrow _____ 5 remember_____ 6 ugly _____

7 dull _____ 8 near _____ 9 late _____

B Write a **synonym** for each of these words.

1 tiny _____ 2 large _____ 3 begin _____

4 stare _____ 5 pretty _____ 6 swiftly _____

7 tired _____ 8 discover _____ 9 shut _____

C Use a thesaurus to help you write four synonyms for each of these words.

1 laugh _____

2 said _____

3 get _____

4 fight _____

D By using prefixes, write the antonym for each of these words.

1 responsible _____

2 probable _____

3 necessary _____

4 legal _____

Published by Thomas Nelson and Sons Ltd 1995

Verbs

> **Verbs** are *action* ('doing') or *being* words.
> Examples: Lizzie *ran* up the hill.
> She *is* here.

A Draw a neat circle round the verb in each of these sentences.

1 Jan ran home.

2 Check your change carefully.

3 The snow blew in my face.

4 Their house is white.

5 There are six of us.

6 Our school has a swimming pool.

> Sometimes we need more than one verb to make a sentence work properly. We need to use **auxiliary verbs** ('helper' verbs) to help the **main verb**.
>
> Examples: Lizzie **had** *run* a long way.
>
> She **will** *run* home again later.
>
> Here are some verbs which can be used as **auxiliary verbs**:
>
> | am | are | is | was | were | be | has | have |
> | had | do | does | did | can | could | may | might |
> | | shall | should | will | would | | | |

B Underline the **main verb** and circle the **auxiliary verb** which is helping it in each of these sentences.

1 Mum and Dad are decorating the bathroom.

2 Mum is washing down the ceiling.

3 Dad has painted the window.

4 He has kicked over the paint.

5 I can see Mum's face.

6 She is giggling to herself!

Tips for better spelling: 10

To make plurals of most nouns that end in **o** we add **es**.

Example: one volcan**o**   two volcano**es**

Beware! There are several important exceptions.

Examples: photos   hippos   radios   rhinos

Music words and words ending in **oo** are also exceptions, so just **add s** to make them plural.

Examples: one pian**o**   two piano**s**

one cuck**oo**   two cuckoo**s**

A   Write the plural of each of these words.

1 hero _____   2 tomato _____

3 potato _____   4 torpedo _____

5 photo _____   6 cockatoo _____

7 cargo _____   8 studio _____

9 cello _____   10 echo _____

The great dinosaur mystery

**Skills Book
Aims:**

1 To further practise use of a
   thesaurus.

2 To practise adding words,
   phrases and clauses to
   enhance a piece of writing.

3 To encourage the use of
   more meaningful words than
   nice, lot, bit and *got.*

4 To practise a further 30
   'tricky' words.

Teaching notes

Stimulus	information text; photographs; illustrations	At this age pupils should be encouraged to move beyond the superficial fascination which so many have with dinosaurs, and to begin considering some of the more fundamental scientific aspects of the subject. Both the stimulus passage and the quiz seek to encourage this in a way that can be extended in many directions, depending on interest levels and access to information sources.
Comprehension	literal; inferential; extension activities	Literal and inferential interpretation are required in Part A, and extension writing-based activities linked to the text and illustrations are offered in Part B.
Vocabulary	using a thesaurus	This section gives further thesaurus practice, which can easily be extended by writing on a board further words to research, together with bland sentences in which individual words might be 'improved'.
Grammar	adding words, phrases and clauses; improving sentences	This section follows naturally from the previous one, extending the concept of enhancing one's writing by the addition and modification of groups of words as well as individual words. **Pcm 1** offers extension and revision of earlier work on adjective and adverb phrases, and on distinguishing between phrases and clauses.
Spelling	"Thirty tricky words"	Suggest that those children who find any of these thirty words difficult might add the words to their personal dictionaries or word lists.
Quiz	odd-one-out	This quiz is much less difficult than the long and daunting names might suggest. However, it does require access to a reasonably well-illustrated reference book or encyclopedia.

See also: **p. 111, Development** notes.

Skills
Unit 12

Comprehension

A 1 'Dinosaur' is Greek for 'terrible lizard'.

2 A vegetarian is an animal or person that does not eat meat.

3 Dinosaurs are described as 'lords of the Earth' because they were the most important and powerful living creatures of their time.

4 The main possible reasons why the dinosaurs became extinct are (a) that the climate changed; (b) that other animals ate their eggs; (c) that the Earth was showered with deadly X-rays; or (d) that huge meteorites collided with the Earth, sending up clouds of dust which blocked the sun and prevented the growth of the plants which the dinosaurs used as food.

B 1 extraordinary – incredible, unusual, unbelievable, etc.
devastating – destructive, shattering, disastrous, etc.
resolve – solve, answer, decide, etc.
significant – important, relevant, etc.
origin – source, starting point
collided – smashed, knocked, crashed, banged, etc. (into)

2 (Individual answers.)

Vocabulary – using a thesaurus

A (Individual answers.)

Vocabulary – improving sentences

Possible answers include:

A 1 I had/received/was given quite a shock/a slight shock.

2 Many of us were looking at the interesting/fascinating/wonderful exhibits.

3 They looked attractive/well displayed, though there were a large number/many/there was a huge collection of them.

4 I, and many/most of my friends, became pretty/fairly tired.

5 One of the dinosaurs had an interesting/a pleasant face.

6 Many/Most of us were drawing it.

7 We are sure it gave us a little/tiny/half smile.

8 Imagine the shock we received/felt/experienced!

9 Dad said it was an amusing/entertaining story – but he didn't believe a word/syllable of it!

Grammar

(Individual answers.)

Spelling

1 recognise
2 miniature
3 separate
4 because
5 library
6 shepherd
7 parliament
8 conscious
9 cupboard
10 encourage
11 happiness
12 burglar
13 excellent
14 justice
15 jewel
16 neighbour
17 villain
18 receive
19 cushion
20 admission
21 addition
22 grudge
23 presence
24 miserable
25 photograph
26 choir
27 column
28 obstinate
29 awkward
30 obstacle

Quiz

1 tyrannosaurus – short neck, meat eater; others vegetarians with long necks

2 brachiosaurus – very large; others much smaller

3 stegosaurus – moves on four legs; others move on two

See also: **p. 111, Development** notes.

Phrases and clauses

Phrases and **clauses** are small groups of words that work together in a sentence.

Clauses have a proper verb, but phrases don't.

An **adjective phrase** is a small group of words that tells us more about a *noun* in a sentence.

> Examples: He was pleased with his new *encyclopedia* **with its twenty volumes**.
>
> (**adjective phrase** about the *encyclopedia* – *a noun*)

An **adverb phrase** is a small group of words that tells us more about a *verb* in a sentence.

> Example: He *ran* **as fast as he could**.
>
> (**adverb phrase** about how he *ran* – *a verb*)

A   Underline one phrase in each sentence and write **adjective phrase** or **adverb phrase** after it.

1 He flicked through all the pages, with their clear and colourful illustrations.   _____

2 The bookshelf, already nearly full, seemed that it might collapse under the weight.   _____

3 He woke bright and early, and went straight to his new books. _____

Clauses are small groups of words similar to **phrases**, except clauses contain a **verb**.

> Examples: The teacher stood up and read the class a story.
>
> This sentence has two verbs and two clauses:
>> 1 The teacher *stood* up
>> 2 and *read* the class a story.

B   Underline the two clauses in different colours in each of these sentences, and neatly circle the verbs.

1 Mr Painter stopped reading until we were all listening.

2 He read in an interesting way and made the characters seem real.

3 I can't wait until tomorrow when we will hear the next chapter.

Published by Thomas Nelson and Sons Ltd 1995

Dragons – fact or fiction?

**Skills Book
Aims:**

1 **To describe puns.**

2 **To revise abstract nouns
and idioms.**

3 **To consider how prefixes
and suffixes can form
nouns, adjectives, verbs
and adverbs.**

4 **To revise and practise the '*i*
before *e*' rule.**

Teaching notes

Stimulus	information text; poem; illustrations	This unit might stimulate much creative craft and art work as well as written work. Different cultures have had their own classic dragons. Possibly invite groups to research and creatively depict different dragons.
Comprehension	literal; inferential	There are literal and inferential questions, and vocabulary extension tasks.
Vocabulary	puns	Start a puns book in which members of the class record and, where appropriate, illustrate puns they have heard or can make up. Perhaps offer a small prize for the best.
Grammar	abstract nouns; idioms; parts of speech	Ensure that dictionaries are available and are used during the exercise on abstract nouns and idioms. The section on parts of speech focuses on how prefixes and suffixes can form nouns, adjectives, verbs and adverbs.
Spelling	Tips for better spelling, 11	*i* comes before *e* except after *c*. The rule is practised, and the many exceptions considered. **Pcm 1** offers further support if needed.
Quiz	word selection	'**Missing Explorers**' is essentially a cloze procedure activity, with a difference.

See also: **p. 113, Development** notes.

Skills
Unit 13

Answers

Comprehension

A 1 Komodo dragons are found on a small group of islands to the east of Java in Indonesia.
  2 They belong to the lizard family.
  3 The pterodactyl is the only reptile thought to have had wings.
  4 Leave it alone and stay at a distance to observe it.

B 1 emblem – symbol, mascot, sign
  2 portrayed – drawn, painted, depicted, shown, described
  3 reptilian – like that of a reptile
  4 depicted – described, painted, portrayed, etc.
  5 dynasty – period when a particular family ruled
  6 infinite – immeasurable, endless, limitless
  7 cache – hoard, store, treasure collection
  8 severing – cutting or breaking through by biting, tearing etc.

Vocabulary

A 1 'Dyeing' sounds like 'dying' and therefore makes you think of the opposite of 'living'.
  2 'Feat' sounds like 'feet', which are what the marathon runner used to perform his feat!
  3 'Alight' means 'get off', but it sounds as if the passengers were on fire!
  4 'Route' sounds like 'root', and a potato is a root vegetable grown in large quantities in Ireland.
  5 'Ancient Greece' sounds like 'ancient grease', which is what these old candles are made of.
  6 Hinges and handles are things which you would find on 'adore' (a door).

Grammar – abstract nouns and idioms

A   (Individual study.)

B 1 cowardice
  2 boastfulness
  3 disgrace
  4 boldness
  5 submission
  6 selfishness
  7 indecision
  8 hypocrisy

C   (Individual answers.)

D   (Individual answers.)

Grammar – parts of speech

reliability	reliable	rely	reliably
playfulness	playful	play	playfully
irritation/ irritability	irritable	irritate	irritably
pity	pitiful	pity	pitifully
agreement	agreeable	agree	agreeably
boast(fulness)	boastful	boast	boastfully
satisfaction	satisfying	satisfy	satisfactorily
amazement	amazing	amaze	amazingly

Spelling

A 2 *ee* sounds: receive, field, believe, wield, deceit, chief, shield, receipt, achieve
  3 **ei** words: receive, deceit, receipt
  4 They all have a **c** before the **ei**.
  5 They are all spelt **ie**.

Quiz

The completed letter could read:
If anyone finds this letter please be <u>VERY</u> careful not to get lost in the same way as I did. Tell my dear husband/wife/ friends that I will never stop trying to escape from the dragons' lair/cave. We were travelling through the dense undergrowth when our leader came upon the cave mouth from which were coming strange noises. The noise we heard was awful and suddenly crashing through the undergrowth came a huge, horrifying dragon. I must stop now for I think I can hear him.

See also: **p. 113, Development** notes.

name _____   date _____

Tips for better spelling: 11

> **i** comes before **e** (when the sound is *ee*)
>   Examples: piece,   relieve,   priest
>
> **except** after **c**
>   Examples: receive,   ceiling,   deceive
>
> **or**   when the sound is *not ee*
>   Examples: reign,   veil,   heir

A   Sort these words into the correct boxes.

receive	field	believe	wield	weigh	eight
their	deceit	rein	chief	shield	vein	receipt
sleight	leisure	achieve	foreign	heir	veil
ceiling	deceive	priest	piece	relieve	thief
height	weight	pier	conceit	relieve

i comes before **e** (when the sound is *ee*)	**except** after **c**	**or** the sound is *not ee*

Spelling rules don't always work in every case – if in doubt, check in a dictionary!

Published by Thomas Nelson and Sons Ltd 1995

Cliffs under attack

1 To give practice in word definition.

2 To introduce the device of word webs.

3 To revise letter layout and punctuation.

4 To revise spelling implications of adding a prefix.

5 To practise selecting antonyms and synonyms.

Teaching notes

Stimulus	information text; photographs; diagram	The main agents effecting coastal erosion are immediately evident, which makes shoreline development a good place to start when considering 'geomorphology' with this age group. Extend the topic by considering (if possible) coastlines with which some or all of the children will be familiar, and also by arranging to look at nearby landscape features (hills, rivers, etc.) and considering their relationships. This, for most children, will be the first time that they have considered how these features have influenced settlement and transport patterns in the area.
Comprehension	literal; extension activities	Part A requires literal interpretation of the information in the text, photographs and diagram, whilst Part B provides opportunities for extension, with revision of onomatopoeia, similes and metaphor.
Vocabulary	definitions; word webs	The work on definitions is an extension of earlier work, giving an introduction to simple etymological principles. Word webs have been introduced earlier in the course, but they are revised here to remind children of the value of giving careful thought and attention to the selection of suitable words when writing. Clearly, the technique might be applied to any topic about which the child is writing.
Punctuation	personal letters; formal (business) letters	Practising letter layout and punctuation can hardly be overdone! Being able to communicate as effectively as possible in both personal and business letters is likely to be one of the most significant and potentially valuable writing skills we can bequeath to most children. Thus it is strongly recommended that opportunities are constantly sought to encourage frequent letter writing. Standards of presentation as well as content should be closely monitored.
Spelling	Tips for better spelling, 12	Prefixes and suffixes causing double letters. **Pcm 1** supports with additional exercises.
Quiz	antonyms and synonyms	This quiz on word pairs offers the opportunity to practise finding antonyms and synonyms. **Pcm 2** provides another quiz on antonyms and synonyms. Each quiz might easily be replicated, with the children creating similar challenges for each other.

See also: **p. 115, Development** notes.

Answers

Comprehension

A 1 The colour of sand on a beach is often the same colour as the rocks or cliffs nearby.

2 If the waves and currents are especially powerful, they can carry away the rocks as soon as they are broken off from the cliffs.

3 Caves in sea cliffs are usually formed where the rocks are slightly weaker than the surrounding cliff.

4 After a cave roof collapses, it can leave an arch of rock, and when the arch separates from the cliff it leaves a sea stack.

B (Individual answers.)

Vocabulary – definitions

A 1 marina – a place next to a river or the sea where pleasure boats may be kept

2 mariner – a person who makes their living by sailing a boat; a sailor

3 maritime – having something to do with the sea

4 submarine – under the sea (adjective); a type of metal boat which can travel under the sea as well as on top of it (noun)

5 submariner – a sailor on a submarine

6 aquamarine – having a bluish-green colour, like the sea (adjective); this colour (noun); a gemstone with this colour (noun)

B (Individual answers.)

Vocabulary – word webs

(Individual answers.)

Punctuation

A

23 Centre Crescent
Blaxland
Essex

15th July

Dear Grandma,
The holiday is almost here! Mum and I already have our coach seats booked and we can't wait to see you.

Do you remember last year when we all went for that long walk along the beach towards Fisherman's Cove, paddling as we went? It was great fun at first but it was really frightening when that large portion of cliff gave way with no warning. It was a wonder that no one on the beach was killed. We were all very lucky. I don't think we'll go there this year, do you?

Well, that's enough for now. I still have to finish some work in time for school tomorrow. Please give my love to Aunty Sue and Uncle Alan and tell my cousins that I'm really excited about seeing them again soon. I can hardly wait!

With love,

Freya

B

23 Centre Crescent
Blaxland
Essex

10th September

To:
The Chief Executive
Beachville Council
Overdown Road
Beachville
Northshire

Dear Sir/Madam,

I should like to make a complaint about the dangerous state of the cliffs near Fisherman's Cove.

When I was walking along the beach with my grandmother yesterday we were very nearly hit by a large rock falling from the cliffs. Whilst I accept that the Council cannot prevent the collapse of the cliffs I do think it is important, and certainly the Council's responsibility, to ensure that there are warning signs in the area.

I look forward to hearing what you intend to do about this situation, which my grandmother and I consider a matter of great urgency.

Yours faithfully,

Freya Smith

Spelling

A 1 dissatisfy, dissimilar

2 unnecessary, unnumbered, unnatural, unnamed

3 overreach, override, overrule, overrun

4 immodest, immeasurable, immoral, immortal, immovable

Quiz

shout – yell (S), whisper (A)
sudden – quick (S), gradual (A)
climb – ascend (S), descend (A)
certain – sure (S), doubtful (A)
protect – safeguard (S), attack (A)

See also: **p. 115, Development** notes.

name _____ date _____

Tips for better spelling: 12

> When **adding a prefix**, *'Just add it!'*.
> Don't miss out any letters.
>   Examples: un + sure = unsure
>   dis + satisfy = di**ss**atisfy
>
> If a matching pair of letters is made by bringing together the last letter of the prefix and the first letter of the word, *don't* be tempted to take one of them out.

A   Underline the correct spelling from the options in brackets.

1   I was (disatisfied, dissatisfied) with my drawing.

2   The twins are (dissimilar, disimilar) to each other.

3   The barn was (overun, overrun) with mice.

4   It is (unnecessary, unecessary) to (override, overide) the system.

5   The heavy log was (imovable, immovable).

B   Choose a **prefix** to make the antonym (opposite) of these words. Use a dictionary to check your answers.

1 obey _____   2 necessary _____

3 moral _____   4 modest _____

5 named _____   6 trust _____

7 possible _____   8 natural _____

9 correct _____   10 legal _____

C   Underline the error in each sentence, and write the correct version at the end.

1 It was inpossible to save enough from his pocket money. _____

2 Have you enough imformation? _____

3 We need ensurance for our holiday in France. _____

4 Her behaviour is inacceptable. _____

Word selection

Complete these sentences.

1   Go is to come as safe is to _____ .

2   Black is to white as visible is to _____ .

3   Husband is to wife as obey is to _____ .

4   Rough is to smooth as possible is to _____ .

5   Here is to there as sense is to _____ .

6   Day is to night as correct is to _____ .

7   Right is to wrong as legal is to _____ .

8   Work is to play as sure is to _____ .

9   Land is to sea as necessary is to _____ .

10   Happy is to sad as trust is to _____ .

11   Good is to bad as please is to _____ .

12   Big is to little as like is to _____ .

Skills
Unit 15

Skills Book Aims:

1 To revise and practise collective nouns.

2 To practise all the punctuation marks hitherto introduced in the course.

3 To introduce 'simple', 'compound' and 'complex' sentences.

4 To practise another 30 key 'tricky' spellings.

5 To provide dictionary activities.

Lions – the cat facts

Teaching notes		
Stimulus	information text; fact file; illustrations	The final unit is linked to cats because this group of animals was the one identified by market research as the group most appealing to young people. Indeed, this is the reason for our series logo! There are many avenues of research and extension work which might be explored by individuals or groups, looking at both wild and domestic cats. Cat books abound, and the class might produce its own anthology of cat writings, including poetry, fairy stories, etc.
Comprehension	literal; multiple-choice; extension activities	Part A offers multiple-choice comprehension of a literal nature, and Part B suggests deductive and extension activities.
Vocabulary	collective nouns	The activity lists some of the more common collective nouns. Others might be collected as an informal activity involving parents and friends.
Punctuation	punctuation marks revision	This activity includes all the main marks except the semi-colon, which all but a very few children will find difficult to assimilate properly until their writing has become rather more sophisticated. **Pcm 1** gives extra practice in the use of contractions and apostrophes, one of the most notoriously difficult areas of punctuation for many people.
Grammar	types of sentence	The unit introduces simple, compound and complex sentences and revises clauses, all of which are practised further in **pcms 2** and **3**.
Spelling	"Another thirty tricky words"	As before, it is suggested that any of the words causing difficulty should be added to personal dictionaries or word lists.
Quiz	cat and dictionary quiz	'**A word cattery**' provides some dictionary fun to finish the course.

See also: **p. 117, Development** notes.

Answers

Comprehension

A 1 roar; lie down
  2 ten thousand
  3 lion; sun; mane
  4 Asian; north-west

B 1 sacred, revered, golden,
     invincible power and
     kingship, bravery,
     masculinity, watchfulness,
     courage, generosity,
     strength, well-equipped
     sight, sensitive to sound,
     aloofness, self-
     confidence, invincibility
  2,3 (Individual answers.)

Vocabulary

A 1 troop
  2 herd
  3 peal
  4 gaggle
  5 pack
  6 convoy
  7 shoal
  8 brood

Punctuation

A 1 Some say the lion is the
     king of the jungle, which is
     strange, because lions in
     Africa, as well as the few
     remaining in India, don't
     live in the jungle.

  2 "Have you ever visited
     Africa?" asked Tom.
  3 "No, but I would like to,"
     replied Wes.
  4 "What is a lion's favourite
     meal?" asked Sundip.
  5 Mr Simmons said that he
     wasn't sure.
  6 "All the lions I've ever
     seen," interjected Tom,
     "seem to love raw meat."
  7 "Hey, just look at that!"
     exclaimed Mr Simmons,
     as he spotted the lions'
     ranger bringing their food.
     "Can you see all that
     meat?"
  8 "That should keep them
     well fed for a while,"
     remarked Wes.
  9 "Speaking of food," said
     Sundip, "isn't it time we
     stopped for lunch?"
 10 As he ate, Sundip listed all
     the creatures they had
     seen so far: elephants,
     giraffes, monkeys, snakes,
     bears and of course, best
     of all, the lions.

Grammar

A (Individual answers.)

B (Individual answers.)

C 1 The River Nile is flooded
     and silts are left behind
     afterwards.

  2 Lions cannot smell things
     very well but they have
     excellent hearing.
  3 This may be an African
     lion or it may be an Asian
     one.

D 1 There are some lions left
     in Asia, but they are found
     only in north-west India.
  2 All cats were worshipped
     in Egypt, and lions were
     particularly sacred.
  3 Lions are very efficient
     hunters but they need to
     be protected from
     humans.

Spelling

A 1 maintenance
  2 caterpillar
  3 vacuum
  4 raspberry
  5 auxiliary
  6 independence
  7 hygienic
  8 mistletoe
  9 parallel
 10 aspirin
 11 restaurant
 12 February
 13 exhaust
 14 exhibition
 15 suitable
 16 definite
 17 acquire
 18 messenger
 19 intention
 20 physical
 21 boundary
 22 incident
 23 maintain
 24 thorough
 25 plague
 26 league
 27 disaster
 28 military
 29 squirrel
 30 postpone

Quiz
  2 catkin
  3 catfish
  4 cathedral
  5 catalogue
  6 catch
  7 caterpillar
  8 catamaran
  9 catnap
 10 cattle

See also: **p. 117, Development** notes. 81

Contractions

> **Contractions** are used in place of two words.
>
> Example: *It's* is a **contraction** of *it is*.
>
> *Don't* is a **contraction** of *do not*.
>
> **Contractions** are usually made by leaving out some letters and putting **an apostrophe** (') in their place.

A Write these contractions out in full.

1 I'll _____   2 I've _____   3 you'll _____

4 they'll _____   5 we're _____   6 it's _____

7 I'm _____   8 doesn't _____   9 don't _____

10 isn't _____   11 wouldn't _____   12 they're _____

B Write the contractions of these words.

1 she will _____   2 they are _____   3 could not _____

4 had not _____   5 who is _____   6 I will _____

7 I have _____   8 they have _____   9 you are _____

10 are not _____   11 will not _____   12 it is _____

C In each of these sentences there are pairs of words that can be made into contractions. Underline each pair, then write the contraction they can make on the line below.

1 They are racing to see who is the fastest sprinter.

_____

2 It is obvious we are in for an exciting event.

_____

3 I do not know which I would expect to win.

_____

SKILLS BOOK 5

Unit 15
ENGLISH **Pcm 2**

name _____ date _____

Types of sentence, 1:
Simple sentences **and** *compound sentences*

> **Simple sentences** have a **single subject** and a **single predicate**.
>
> Example: The girls / are hungry.
>   subject   predicate

A   Add a *subject* or *predicate* to complete these as **simple sentences**.

1 The old lady _____ .

2 _____ ran from the burning wreck.

3 A pack of dogs _____ .

> **Compound sentences** are made up from *two or more simple sentences* joined by a **conjunction**, such as *and, but, or*.
>
> Example: The girls / are hungry.   (simple sentence)
>   subject   predicate
>
>   Lunch / isn't ready yet.   (simple sentence)
>   subject   predicate
>
> The girls are hungry **but** lunch isn't
> ready yet.   (compound sentence)

B   Make **compound sentences** from these pairs of sentences.

1 Joey likes playing football.
   He is a very skilful player.

   _____

   _____

2 The spaceship orbited the moon for several days.
   Mission Control would not allow them to land.

   _____

   _____

3 I shall probably stay in tonight.
   I might go and visit my Grandma.

   _____

   _____

name _____ date _____

Types of sentence, 2:
Compound sentences **and** *complex sentences*

> **Compound sentences** are made by joining *two simple sentences*.
> **Compound sentences** have **two main clauses**. **Main** clauses are parts of sentences that can stand by themselves.

A Use a ruler to underline the two **main** clauses in these sentences. Draw a circle round the *conjunction* which introduces the second clause.

1 The weather on Saturday was atrocious, but the game was played despite the conditions.

2 There was a huge crowd and there was a tremendous atmosphere inside the ground.

3 Our team won but at half-time we were two goals down.

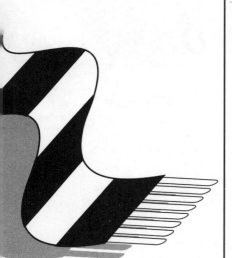

> **Subordinate clauses** *help* **the main clause** but do not make sense without the main clause.
> **Complex sentences** are made by adding a **subordinate** clause to a **main** clause.
>
> Example: There was a huge crowd / willing the teams on.
>   main clause   subordinate clause
>
> *There was a huge crowd*   makes sense by itself. It is therefore a **main** clause.
>
> *willing the teams on.*   does not make sense without the main clause. It is therefore a **subordinate** clause.

B Neatly underline the **main clauses** in blue and the **subordinate clauses** in red in these **complex sentences**.

1 My favourite player is Gilkes, who often scores clever goals.

2 Dad buys burgers at half-time, which keeps us warm on cold days.

3 The manager has bought a new striker who is said to be good in the air.

Vocabulary

A 1 United Nations International Children's Emergency Fund (**or** United Nations Children's Fund)
   2 Oxford Committee for Famine Relief
   3 Royal Society for the Prevention of Accidents

B 1 grandmother – feminine
   2 uncle – masculine
   3 Belfast – neuter
   4 elephant – common
   5 computer – neuter
   6 Jenny – feminine
   7 people – common
   8 monk – masculine

C 1 wake – awaken
   2 honest – dishonesty
   3 perfect – imperfection
   4 appoint – disappointment/ disappointing/disappointed

D either; or; neither; Neither; nor

E 1 stated/shouted/exclaimed/ asserted/retorted/cried etc.
   2 asked/retorted/rejoined/ interjected etc.
   3 repeated/answered/ muttered etc.

Punctuation

A 1 "Would you like to start a computer club at lunchtimes?" asked our teacher.
   2 I asked her how often the club would meet.
   3 "I thought you/we could meet about twice a week," she answered.
   4 I told her/said I was certain that the club would be very popular.

B Miss Jenkins, our teacher, suggested that we call the club the Campbeltown School Computer Club. She said we should make posters to advertise the first meeting. Owen, Ben, Maxine, Janie and I drew five posters. We asked Mrs Smith if we could put them on the head teacher's notice board.

Grammar

A younger – adjective
   pupils – noun
   watched – verb
   intently – adverb
   we – pronoun
   explained – verb
   carefully – adverb
   smart – adjective
   new – adjective
   computers – noun
   worked – verb

B 1 Several children brought their games.
   2 May I borrow your computer?
   3 What is its capacity?
   4 It has a larger capacity than my/his/her machine.

C (Individual answers.)

Spelling

A 1 argument
   2 arguing
   3 safely
   4 shared
   5 caring
   6 careless
   7 humorous
   8 vigorous
   9 beginning
   10 transmitted
   11 boxing
   12 singing

B 1 imaginary
   2 bakery
   3 confectionery
   4 thundery
   5 monastery
   6 machinery
   7 cemetery
   8 stationary/stationery
   9 Number 8; *stationary* means not moving, standing still; *stationery* is a collective noun meaning sheets of paper you write letters on, and envelopes to send them in, etc.

Vocabulary

A 1 hair, hare, have, honour, hope, hopeful, hoping
   2 France, free, freely, French, fresh, friend
   3 man, Manchester, material, maths, matter, mouse

B Different answers are possible; the words in each pair of brackets can be used as alternatives:
   1 London is a (huge)/(big) city.
   2 We were (pleased)/(happy) to have the (chance)/ (opportunity) to go on the (fascinating)/(interesting) visit.
   3 We visited (a lot of)/(many) (interesting) sites (worth seeing).

C 1 mis – not; badly; wrong
   2 anti – against; opposite to
   3 un – not; the opposite to or reverse of
   4 pre – before (time); in front of (position)
   5 sub – under; less than; almost

Punctuation

"Where are we going first?" Jim asked Mr Jake, his teacher.
   "Well," came the reply, "that all depends on the traffic. If we get to central London before about eleven o'clock we can go to the Mall and watch the Welsh Guards changing the guard at Buckingham Palace."
   "What will we do if we miss that?" asked Jim, never short of questions.
   "We shall go straight to see Nelson's Column in Trafalgar Square," retorted the irritated teacher, who was more interested in studying the street map than answering a barrage of questions from young Jim.

Grammar

A 1 curiosity   4 generosity
   2 happiness   5 weakness
   3 jealousy

B 1 This is a worksheet <u>which</u> I want you to complete.
   2 Find a guide <u>which(/who)</u> can help you answer the questions.
   3 Here is your ticket, <u>which</u> you mustn't lose.
   4 There will be a prize for the person <u>who</u> completes the work most thoroughly.

C 1 The sky was lit up by the bright city lights.
   2 The streets were crowded with hundreds of people.
   3 We were taken to Oxford Street by our coach driver.

D 1 We all settled back in our seats.
   2 The coach stopped at the services on the motorway.

Spelling

A 1 impossible
   2 advisable
   3 usable
   4 approachable
   5 negligible
   6 responsible
   7 probable
   8 incredible

B 1 happily   4 cheerily
   2 nastily   5 heavily
   3 merrily

C 1 marshes
   2 watches
   3 foxes
   4 buses
   5 grasses
   6 ponies
   7 roofs
   8 days
   9 difficulties
   10 curries
   11 wives
   12 wolves
   13 loaves
   14 halves
   15 thieves

D 1 irreplaceable
   2 torrential
   3 polluting; atmosphere

A 1 huge: (S) big, large, enormous, great, vast, etc; (A) tiny, little, minuscule, small, minute, etc.

2 wide: (S) vast, broad, etc; (A) narrow, tight, constricted, thin, etc.

3 beautiful: (S) pretty, gorgeous, splendid, attractive, etc; (A) ugly, horrible, plain, etc.

4 kind: (S) generous, helpful, caring, etc; (A) unkind, cruel, rotten, horrible, etc.

5 difficult: (S) hard, awkward, tough, etc; (A) easy, simple, straightforward, etc.

6 healthy: (S) well, fit, strong, etc; (A) unhealthy, sick, ill, poor, bad, etc.

7 rare: (S) valuable, uncommon, scarce, etc; (A) common, ordinary, frequent, etc.

8 puzzle: (S) conundrum, competition, riddle, difficulty, etc; (A) anything obvious or easy

B The young man in his tatty <u>cardigan</u> played his <u>saxophone</u> as we sat on my <u>mackintosh</u> eating our <u>sandwiches</u>.

C 1 litter
2 pride
3 flock
4 shoal
5 herd

Punctuation

A Jungles can be strange, eerie, yet fascinating places. Shafts of light cut through the high green canopy to the damp, misty, gloomy floor below. There's the constant noise of monkeys squawking and chattering, birds calling and screeching, and the incessant drip, drip, drip of water falling through the high leaves and creepers onto the mat of smelly, decaying vegetation. It's not surprising that most people find jungles hostile environments best left to the wild animals and birds.

B "Do you realise," enquired Anita, "that there are over seventy countries in the world with some jungle areas?"

"I'm surprised there are that many," replied Mark, "I thought all the rainforests were being destroyed."

"Yes, you're right," she said. "Unfortunately, a space large enough for 60 football pitches is cleared every minute. Once, the rainforest area was much larger than it is today. It's a terrible problem."

C (Individual answers.)

Grammar

A 1 ran
2 sitting
3 drank
4 begun
5 taken
6 were

B (Individual answers.)

C 1 We received/had a (minor/little/terrible) fright when we heard the howl.
2 Every one/All of us climbed into/climbed aboard/ boarded the minibus.
3 We soon realised the animals were harmless/friendly/ interesting, but you had/needed to be slightly/fairly/a little careful.
4 The pleasant/kindly/friendly old lady was bitten lots of times/suffered many bites from mosquitos/many mosquito bites.

D (Individual answers.)

Noun	Adjective	Verb	Adverb
E irritability	irritable	irritate	irritably
play(fulness)	playful	play	playfully
fright	frightening	frighten	frighteningly
boast(fulness)	boastful	boast	boastfully

Spelling

A 1 radios
2 tomatoes
3 volcanoes or volcanos
4 cuckoos
5 cellos
6 echoes
7 pianos
8 cockatoos
9 boxes
10 sheep
11 glasses
12 cherries
13 chiefs
14 cars
15 loaves
16 women

B 1 villain
2 separate
3 choir
4 burglar
5 obstacle
6 miniature
7 recognise
8 awkward

C 1 receive
2 conceit
3 wield
4 rein
5 achieve
6 their
7 mischief
8 receipt

D 1 unnecessary
2 override
3 immovable
4 dissimilar
5 untidy
6 immeasurable

E 1 keenness
2 goalless
3 suddenness

F 1 exhibition
2 auxiliary
3 suitable
4 league
5 parallel
6 raspberry
7 February
8 acquire

Development Book 5 **Scope and Sequence**

Unit	Stimulus	Comprehension*	Writing	Personal choice
1 **City life**	famous painting; modern fiction; modern poetry	famous painting; modern fiction; modern poetry	observing and recording – descriptive; research; drafting and redrafting	pros and cons; descriptive writing; narrative writing; research – fact file
2 **Victorian times**	classic children's fiction; modern children's fiction	classic children's fiction; modern children's fiction	characterisation; drafting and redrafting	factual writing; opinions; narrative writing
3 **Do you believe in ghosts?**	modern fiction; modern poetry	modern fiction; Poetry Study	narrative; descriptive; drafting and redrafting	imaginative writing; personal opinion; personal experience
4 **Other worlds**	modern fiction; modern poetry	modern fiction	narrative; conversation	book cover; diary
5 **Advertising**	advertisements – past and present; information text	advertisements	persuasive language; layout; visual appeal; comparisons	personal opinion; factual writing; advertisement
6 **The unsinkable** *Titanic*	newspaper report; eye-witness account; factual texts	eye-witness account; newspaper report	imaginative – eye-witness account; imaginative – reported account; research – factual account; drafting and redrafting	personal letter; interviews; research – graphic presentation
7 **Jamaica**	map; photographs; charts; factual text; tables	map; charts; factual text; tables	persuasive writing; filling in forms; business letters	travel poster; personal letter; factual – graphic presentation
8 **Night**	modern poetry; traditional verse	Poetry Study	writing poetry; similes and metaphors	descriptive writing; personal opinion; narrative writing
9 **Extinction!**	modern fiction; factual text; modern poetry	modern fiction; modern poetry	discursive writing; drafting and redrafting	narrative writing; poster; discursive writing
10 **Life in the factories**	factual text; modern poetry	factual text; modern poetry	summaries; personal opinion; discursive writing	imaginative writing; advertisement; personal writing
11 **Moral tales**	traditional tale; traditional poetry; fables	traditional tale; traditional poetry; fables	comparisons – analysis; personal response; fables	playscript; fable
12 **Mystery of the** *Mary Celeste*	factual texts; traditional verse	factual text	narrative – mystery stories; personal response	book cover/blurb writing; factual report; poetry
13 **Weird and wonderful**	modern fiction; poetry	modern fiction	playscript; personal response	narrative writing; personal letter; poetry
14 **Danger on the cliff**	modern fiction; book reviews	modern fiction; book review	prediction; continuing a narrative; book reviews	book cover/blurb writing; conversation
15 **Cats**	factual text; modern poetry; traditional fiction	factual text	comparisons – purpose and audience; various styles of writing; a book or wall display	factual writing; personal writing; narrative writing; descriptive writing

*NOTE: Comprehension may be literal and/or inferential

City life

1 **To use personal experience and circumstances as a basis for writing.**

2 **To encourage detailed observation and recording.**

Marking suggestion

Teachers may choose to paste photocopies of the unit answers on to cards and store these in a simple box, so the children can check their own answers, as appropriate.

Each card should be clearly labelled with the book title and unit number and title, to enable the children to find and use the correct unit answers easily.

Teaching notes

Stimulus	famous painting	*Market Scene, Northern Town, 1939* by Lowry. It would be useful to show the children other paintings by Lowry. What do they notice about the paintings? Do they like them? Do they convey the impression of busy city life?
Comprehension	literal; inferential	The children are required to analyse the painting in terms of audience response. Question 4 asks for an imaginative leap based on the two characters in the foreground. Discuss the concepts of 'background' and 'foreground'.
Stimulus	modern fiction	*Sandra Street* by Michael Anthony. This passage moves the unit's theme of urban life into another part of the world and introduces the idea of looking at and describing familiar surroundings.
Comprehension	literal; inferential	The questions concentrate on the feelings of the narrator and characters for their surroundings.
Writing	observing and recording	The children are required to observe and record the details of their own surroundings as well as their feelings about where they live. The idea of brainstorming is introduced along with word webs as a device for recording their ideas.
Stimulus	modern poetry	*Trip to London* by Leonard Clark. Have the children ever visited London? Did they see any of the sights mentioned in the poem? Have some pictures of Trafalgar Square, Hyde Park, etc. available for the children to look at.
Comprehension	inferential	The questions again concentrate on the writer's feelings towards a city, but this time from the perspective of someone who lives in the countryside.
Writing	research; drafting and redrafting	Ensure that the children have access to suitable reference books, encyclopedias and guide books for this task. Some children might research famous London sights that are not mentioned in the poem. Encourage the children to draft and redraft their work. It could be word processed and illustrated to form a classroom display around a map of London. **Pcm 1** – London. This gives specific areas of research for Buckingham Palace and Trafalgar Square.
Personal choice		**Pcm 2** – Personal choice, a grid in which the children can record the type of writing they choose from the Personal choice section in each unit. The options here are: 1 pros and cons; 2 descriptive writing; 3 narrative writing; 4 research – fact file.

Answers

Picture study – *Market Scene, Northern Town, 1939*

Individual answers reflecting the individual child's response to the painting.

Comprehension – *Sandra Street*

1 Individual answers.
2 dull and uninteresting/ wilderness/so different from our other streets
3 Sandra Street
4 The other side of town had 'gay attractions' and space for playing cricket and football.

5 The narrator likes Sandra Street because it is his home.
6 savannah
7 Individual answers.

Comprehension – *Trip to London*

1 busy, wet, noisy, lots to see and do
2 He likes the peace of the countryside and the fact that it is familiar to him.

3 He prefers the 'country things', such as the trees, hills and birds, to the noise and bustle of the city.
4 Everything moves at such a fast pace in the city.

See also: **p. 24, Skills** notes.

Nelson
ENGLISH

DEVELOPMENT BOOK 5
Unit 1
Pcm 1

name _____ date _____

London

1 Who lives here?
2 When was it built?
3 Why is it called Buckingham Palace?
4 When was it rebuilt?

1 What statue can be found in Trafalgar Square?
2 What was he famous for?
3 How high is the column?
4 Why is this area of London called Trafalgar Square?

Published by Thomas Nelson and Sons Ltd 1995

name _____ date _____

Personal choice

CHOICES \ UNITS	1	2	3	4	5	6	7	8	9	10	11	12	13	14	15
pros and cons	A1														
descriptive writing	A2							A1							
narrative writing	A3	A3						A3	A1				A1		
research – fact file	A4														
factual writing		A1			A3	A3	A3					A2			
opinions		A2	A2		A1/2			A2							
imaginative writing			A1							A1					
personal writing			A3							A3			A2		
book covers				A1								A1		A1	
diary				A2											
advertisments					A4					A2					
personal letters						A1	A2								
interviews						A2									
posters							A1	A2							
discursive writing								A3							
playscripts											A1				
fables											A2				
poetry													A3	A3	
conversation														A2	

(WHOLE UNIT = PERSONAL CHOICE)

Key: A means Assignment
Colour the square for each assignment you have done.

Published by Thomas Nelson and Sons Ltd 1995

Nelson English © John Jackman and Wendy Wren 1995.

Development Unit 2

Victorian times

Development Book Aims:

1 **To look at characterisation in fiction.**

Teaching notes		
Stimulus	classic children's fiction	*A Christmas Carol* by Charles Dickens.
Comprehension	literal; inferential	**Characters in stories** The children are required to analyse what they have learned about the character of Scrooge in these extracts, both through direct authorial description and the character's conversation.
Stimulus	classic children's fiction	*The Water Babies* by Charles Kingsley. This is the opening of the novel where the author tells the reader about Tom.
Comprehension	literal	The children are required to write down what they know about Tom after reading the passage, and to decide which method the author has used to communicate this knowledge to them, i.e. direct authorial comment or character's speech and action. Ask the children to pick out passages in other books they have read and say how they found out about the characters.
Stimulus	modern children's fiction	*Smith* by Leon Garfield.
Comprehension	literal; inferential	The reader learns about the characters of Smith and the priest through both methods of characterisation. The children are required to write about what they have learned and state which methods have been used. Some discussion about a 'Wanted Poster' would be useful. What is Smith wanted for? Will there be a reward? Why does the description have to be accurate?
Writing	characterisation; drafting and redrafting	**Your own characters** The children are given the plot (a postwoman delivering a parcel) and also a paragraph plan to follow. They can elaborate on the plot and give details of the setting but the main task is to let the reader know what sort of characters are involved. **Pcm 1** – Delivering the parcel, gives one possible outcome based on the characters of the people involved.
Personal choice		The options here are: 1 factual writing; 2 opinions; 3 narrative writing.

Answers

Characters in stories –
A Christmas Carol

1 Individual answers which indicate that Scrooge is mean, miserly, unkind, hard, etc.
2 Individual answers which indicate that Scrooge is humourless, bad tempered and does not join in the general festivities at Christmas.

Characters in stories –
The Water Babies

1 Tom could not read or write; didn't wash; he cried when he had to work and laughed when he was playing. He took all the things that happened to him as 'the way of the world'.
2 What the author has told the reader.

Characters in stories – *Smith*

1 The priest is a man who cannot be fooled. He is proud and does not show Smith any Christian kindness.
2 Smith can act in a charming and innocent way when he wants something and he can lie when it suits his purpose. He can also be very angry and insulting if he doesn't get what he wants.

See also: **p. 32**, Skills notes.

name _____ date _____

Delivering the parcel

Read what the postwoman and the old man say to each other.

What sort of person do you think the postwoman is?

_____

_____

_____

What sort of person do you think the old man is?

_____

_____

_____

Published by Thomas Nelson and Sons Ltd 1995

Do you believe in ghosts?

1 **To continue looking at
different types of narrative
writing – ghost stories.**

Teaching notes

Stimulus	modern fiction	*The Ghost of Thomas Kempe* by Penelope Lively. When the children have worked through the unit, suggest that they read the book to find out what happens.
Comprehension	literal; inferential	Discuss the passage with the children in terms of the different attitudes of Bert and Will to what they are doing. How would they react in James's place? Do they think Bert knows what he is doing?
Writing	narrative; descriptive; drafting and redrafting	**Writing a ghost story** This analysis of the ordinary and unusual things which occur in the passage is designed to show the children that ghost stories do not always take place in ruined, deserted castles with eerie noises and bloodcurdling screams! The method of contrast builds up the suspense and the detail given makes the reader feel that they are witnessing the events. Use **pcm 1** – Story Planning Sheet.
Stimulus	modern poetry	*Two's Company* by Raymond Wilson.
Comprehension	Poetry Study	The special Comprehension area of 'Poetry Study' is introduced in Development Book 5, where a poem is used to trigger ideas rather than for literal or inferential analysis alone. In *Two's Company* suspense is built up by describing a series of unusual things, and this is intended to help the children in their own writing on being alone in a haunted house.
Personal choice		The options here are: 1 imaginative; 2 opinion; 3 personal.

Answers

Comprehension – *The Ghost of Thomas Kempe*

1 He would be nervous because they were trying to trap the ghost and because some member of his family might come in and disturb them.
2 pencil/pieces of paper/rowan stick/curtain ring
3 If the ghost enters the circle Bert will have him in his power.

4 You have to go very carefully and not rush things.
6 wrote – pencilled
searched – rummaged
surprised – startled
stared intensely – riveted

Poetry Study – *Two's Company*

1 hunchback moon
screech-owls calling
chains rattled
someone screamed
stroke of twelve – but there's
  no clock
A voice breathes softly

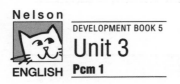

name _____   date _____

Story planning sheet

---

1 Title

---

2 Setting

---

3 Characters

---

4 Plot   **Beginning**

Middle

End

Development
Unit 4

See also: **p. 40**, **Skills** notes.

Development Book Aims:

1 To continue to look at different types of narrative writing – stories set in other worlds.

Teaching notes

Stimulus	modern fiction	*Tom's Midnight Garden* by Philippa Pearce. When the children have worked through the unit, suggest they read the book to find out what happens.
Comprehension	literal; inferential	The questions encourage the children to look closely at the detail of the passage and to appreciate how Tom is feeling and reacting to the strange circumstances.
Writing	narrative	**Stories in other worlds** This gives children the opportunity to write a short story based on the idea in *Tom's Midnight Garden* i.e. going into the past. This could be linked with the particular history topic being studied, which would give the children some factual detail for their story. The 'setting – character – plot' structure forms the basis for narrative writing, as usual, but here the emphasis is on 'setting' as the crucial element. **Pcm 1** – Setting the scene, gives one possible historical time for the children to describe.
Stimulus	modern fiction; modern poetry	*The Snow Spider* by Jenny Nimmo. When the children have worked through the unit, suggest they read the book to find out what happens. The poem included as an additional stimulus is by Kelly Williams and was written as a writing exercise in response to the book *The Snow Spider*.
Comprehension	literal	Reading for understanding as an introduction to another kind of 'other world' story.
Writing	conversation	**Visitors from other worlds** As a contrast to *Tom's Midnight Garden*, *The Snow Spider* has a visitor from another world. The children are required to imagine a conversation between Gwyn and Bethan. Read the poem by Kelly with the children and discuss the sorts of things Gwyn might ask. This work could be extended by having the children write their own story about a visitor from another world. Encourage them to use the idea of a magical world rather than a being from another planet.
Personal choice		The options here are: 1 book cover; 2 diary.

Answers

Comprehension – *Tom's Midnight Garden*

1 Tom hears the grandfather clock striking thirteen.
2 They had said there was no point in going to the back of the house as there was only a small backyard with rubbish bins.
3 Tom would go out into the garden without his aunt and uncle knowing.
4 What was under his feet felt different.
5 Individual answers suggesting that at the stroke of thirteen he was transported back in time.

Comprehension – *The Snow Spider*

1 breathed/whispered
These words convey a sense of surprise and wonder.
2 the impression her elbow made on the arm of the chair/the fibres in her skirt/the lines on her slim, pale hand
3 The girl was the same as his sister in the way she sat and the way she gazed into the fire.
Bethan was dark with rosy cheeks and tanned skin. The girl in the web was fragile and silver-pale.

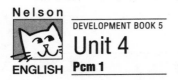
name _____   date _____

Setting the scene

Look at the picture.
Imagine that you have been taken back in time to this place.
Write some words and phrases to describe:

The setting	The people	How you feel
_____	_____	_____
_____	_____	_____
_____	_____	_____
_____	_____	_____
_____	_____	_____
_____	_____	_____
_____	_____	_____
_____	_____	_____
_____	_____	_____

Advertising

1 To introduce the language
of advertising in the context
of persuasive language.

Teaching notes		
Stimulus	advertisements – past and present	**Advertisement for Supermunch Breakfast cereal** Have a variety of magazine advertisements for the children to look at. Discuss the advertisements on television. Which ones can the children remember? Why? Discuss the use of jingles, pop music, use of famous personalities, etc.
Comprehension	literal; inferential	The questions are designed to make the children look closely at the advertisement and think about its appeal. Questions 1–4 can be used to analyse other advertisements.
Stimulus	information text	**The advertiser's job** These notes will help the children to be aware of the things they must consider when they write their own advertisements. They can be used as a basis for analysing other magazine advertisements and writing a report on why the advertisement is successful or not.
Writing	persuasive language; layout; visual appeal; comparisons	**Writing advertisements** Using the information the children have gained about advertisements, they now write their own for two of the four pictures. Encourage them to do rough drafts in pencil with notes to indicate colour, type size, etc. instead of immediately attacking the paper with felt tips! **Pcm 1** – Advertising a car, will help the children to think carefully about the language used.
Comprehension	inferential; literal	**Advertising in the past** This is a comparative comprehension task to help the children understand that the appeal of an advertisement is not everlasting. Can they suggest why the old advertisement looks the way it does? If they prefer the old one can they say why? Do some modern advertisements look old-fashioned? Why?
Personal choice		The options here are: 1 opinion; 2 opinion; 3 factual; 4 advertisement.

Answers

1 Supermunch cereal
2 parents
3 The name of the cereal indicates that it is tasty and the best.
4 vitamins/tasty/fibre/healthy/ the best/good supermarkets
5 This indicates that it is of high quality as only 'good' supermarkets will sell it.
6 Rhyme is used to make you remember it.
7 Individual answers.

DEVELOPMENT BOOK 5

Unit 5

ENGLISH **Pcm 1**

name _____ date _____

Advertising a car

> # This new car is very nice. It is quick and cheap to run. It looks good.

Look at this advertisement. It is not very exciting.
See if you can improve it so that people will want to buy the car.

Think of a name for the car.

_____

Use your thesaurus to find more interesting words for:

nice _____

quick _____

cheap _____

good _____

Write your advertisement here:

_____

_____

_____

_____

_____

_____

Development
Unit 6

The unsinkable *Titanic*

Development Book Aims:

1 **To look at eye-witness and second-hand accounts of the same event.**

Teaching notes

Stimulus	eye-witness account	**A Night to Remember** An eye-witness account of the sinking of the *Titanic*.
Comprehension	inferential	The questions concentrate on the language of the passage. Why was Walter Lord able to describe things so vividly?
Stimulus	newspaper report	Newspaper report of the sinking of the *Titanic*, from the *Daily Herald*.
Comprehension	literal; inferential	The questions concentrate on the events of that night as the reporter would be keen to know exactly what happened.
Writing	imaginative – eye-witness account; imaginative – reported account	1 Here the children are required to analyse the newspaper report and pick out the words and phrases that indicate that the reporter was not personally involved in the incident. This work can be extended orally by having one child relate something in which s/he was personally involved, and another child report the event second-hand. **Pcm 1** – Fire! will give the children further practice. 2 a An imaginative task based on the facts of the stimulus passages. Encourage the children to use vivid descriptions as Walter Lord did, and to include their thoughts and feelings. 2 b This should be the same account as 2a in its factual detail. A reporter would be most interested in 'the facts' because his/her readers would want to know what had actually happened.
Writing	research – factual account; drafting and redrafting	An exercise enabling the children to use information retrieval skills to write a short factual account. Make sure there are suitable reference books and encyclopedias for the children to use. Encourage them to add other information and to draft and redraft their reports rather than just answering the questions. Remind them of the stages involved in this type of work.
Writing	note-taking; opinions	**What's in a name?** This can be used as the basis for a class or group discussion looking at various explanations for the unusual events. Encourage the children to give reasons for the explanation they think most likely.
Personal choice		The options here are: 1 personal letter; 2 interviews; 3 factual – graphic representation.

Answers

Comprehension – *A Night to Remember*

1 The general uproar was caused by people panicking.
2 straight up in the air
3 glistening/the water would be catching what light there was
4 That the *Titanic* would not go down.
5 The night sky was full of stars looking like a typical scene on a Christmas card.

6 starboard – right side of the ship
aft – towards the back (stern) of the ship
hull – frame of the ship
flagstaff – pole on which flag is hung

Comprehension – The *Daily Herald*

1 Mr Stengal was obviously well off as he was travelling in the best part of the ship.
2 It is a custom at sea always to save women and children first.

3 Some of the survivors had heard the crew threaten to shoot the men who were trying to get into the lifeboats.
4 To help to row the boat.
5 The reporter tells the readers that people were 'shrieking' and 'hysterical'.
6 berth – sleeping place on a ship
stern – the back of the ship
gunwale – the upper edge of the boat

Research

4 Southampton
5 America
6 2207
8 April 14th, 1912
9 1513

See also: p. 46, Skills notes.

Fire!

Mr Black is the man being rescued in the picture. Imagine you are Mr Black. Use a sheet of paper to write a letter to a friend explaining what happened and how you felt. Remember to describe everything in detail because you – as Mr Black – were actually there.

Miss White is a reporter for a newspaper.

She interviews Mr Black the day after the fire. She wants to know the facts about the fire. Use a sheet of paper to write her newspaper report.

Remember she wasn't there so she can only write about what Mr Black tells her.

Development
Unit 7

Jamaica

Development Book Aims:

1 To look at persuasive and factual writing in the context of a holiday brochure.

2 To introduce business letters.

Teaching notes

Stimulus	holiday brochure	Holiday brochure layout comprising: factual text; photographs; charts; tables; map.
Comprehension	literal	**Reading for information** Question 2 is slightly different to the rest. It is based on the text on page 40, the aim of which is to persuade the reader that Jamaica is an ideal place to go for a holiday. Can the children see that the facts here are presented in a different way to those on the map or in the Island Information chart?
Writing	persuasive writing	**Writing to persuade** The children are required to analyse the way in which the information is presented on the holiday brochure pages, in terms of how persuasive it is. This could be done in groups and reported back to the class.
Writing	filling in forms	**Booking your holiday** The children use the tables on pp. 42 and 43 to fill in the Booking form, **pcm 1**. To make the exercise as realistic as possible, the children can work in pairs or groups of three or four.
Writing	business letters	**Did you have a good time?** Two opportunities to write business letters within the context of the unit. The points to remember are those taught in **Skills Book 5**, Unit 14. **Pcm 2** – A reply, gives the children the opportunity to write as if they were the manager of the travel company.
Personal choice		The options here are: 1 travel poster; 2 personal letter; 3 factual – graphic presentation.

Answers

Comprehension

1 in the Caribbean
2 beautiful scenery/sports/ relaxation/good weather
3 lush forests/magical plantations/incredible beaches
4 October
5 Montego Bay
6 Kingston
7 84°F
8 North
9 Montego Bay
10 Ocho Rios

See also: p. 49, Skills notes. 101

name _____   date _____

Booking form

SUNSHINE TRAVEL COMPANY | 44 Mill Lane
London
SW20 9XY

NAME OF PERSON BOOKING HOLIDAY: ADDRESS

_____   _____

        _____

        _____

        _____

        TEL. NO. _____

PEOPLE TRAVELLING WITH YOU:
Surname   Initials   Mr/Miss/Mrs/Ms

_____   _____   _____

_____   _____   _____

_____   _____   _____

_____   _____   _____

NAME OF HOTEL: _____

        Please tick

SELF-CATERING: ☐

HOTEL ROOMS: ☐   HOW MANY ROOMS? _____

DATES OF HOLIDAY: FROM _____ TO _____

ANY SPECIAL REQUIREMENTS?

_____

_____

        TOTAL PRICE: _____

10% OF TOTAL PRICE AS DEPOSIT: _____

        SIGNATURE _____

A reply

You are the manager of a travel company. You receive this letter from Mrs Long who has just returned from holiday in Montego Bay.

Primrose Cottage
Sheep Lane
Starbridge
Kent
ZX5 6QS

The Manager
Sunshine Travel Company
44, Mill Lane
London
SW20 9XY

1st August 1995

Dear Sir or Madam,
Having just returned from my holiday in Montego Bay,
I felt I must write to your company to let you know
that I am less than satisfied.

On arrival I found my room at the Seaview Hotel had
been double booked, so I was forced to take a self-
catering apartment.

The rafting trips on the *Martha Brae* were always
fully booked and the hotel swimming pool was far
from clean.

I have paid a considerable sum of money for my
holiday which, I am afraid to say, has been totally
wasted.

Yours faithfully,

Mrs Elsie Long

Mrs Long

Write a reply to Mrs Long.

Published by Thomas Nelson and Sons Ltd 1995

Nelson English © John Jackman and Wendy Wren 1995.

Development
Unit 8

Night

Development Book
Aims:

1 To look at the purposes and
effects of poetry.

Teaching notes

Stimulus	modern poetry	*Night Shapes* by Paddy Kinsale.
Comprehension	inferential	The questions concentrate on the vocabulary the poet has used to convey an eerie, menacing atmosphere.
Stimulus	modern poetry	*Night* by Sergei Esenin.
Comprehension	inferential	Again, the questions concentrate on the vocabulary, this time used to convey a peaceful, safe atmosphere. Question 4 asks the children to say which poem they prefer. This could be done as a class or group discussion.

Comprehension	Poetry Study	**Poetry and purpose**
		    The two stimulus poems are analysed in terms of vocabulary to show the children that the same subject can be treated in different ways.
		    Can they find other pairs of poems on the same subject which achieve very different effects?
		    They could make word webs for the poems to highlight the different use of vocabulary. **Pcm 1** – Point of view, gives them further practice.

Writing	writing poetry	**Writing your own night poem** The notes take the children through some of the things they need to consider when writing a night poem of their own. Obviously there are things such as rhyme, metre, etc. but the authors feel that it is best left to the individual teacher to decide what level the children have reached in their poetry writing.
Stimulus	traditional verse	*The Highwayman* by Alfred Noyes. The children may like to read the whole poem.
Writing	similes and metaphors	Based on the stimulus poem, *The Highwayman*, this exercise gives children practice in the use of similes and metaphors in the context of poetry. They can then use their similes and metaphors to write another poem.
Personal choice		The options here are: 1 descriptive writing; 2 personal opinion; 3 narrative writing.

Answers

Comprehension – *Night Shapes*

1 Individual answers which suggest that the poet feels the night is threatening and eerie.
2 Individual answers.
3 The poet feels that people who are out in the night are strange and secretive.
4 stealing – moving secretively
brooding – hanging closely and sullenly
looming – making a first appearance, often not clearly

Comprehension – *Night*

1 The poet finds night peaceful and safe.
2 level plain with lush grass
3 It turns the landscape to silver.
4 Individual answers.

See also: **p. 55**, **Skills** notes.

name _____ date _____

Point of view

Look at the pictures.

The first one shows a very
stormy sea.

The second one shows someone
on a very high building.

1 Write a description of each picture from the point of view of
   someone who
   a likes being at sea in a storm
   b likes being at the top of a high building.

2 Write a description of each picture from the point of view of
   someone who
   a dislikes being at sea in a storm
   b dislikes being at the top of a high building.

Don't just say 'I like' or 'I don't like'. Choose your descriptive words
carefully so the reader knows your point of view.

Development Book Aims:

1 **To introduce discursive writing.**

Teaching notes		
Stimulus	modern fiction	*Free Willy* by Todd Strasser. Suggest that the children read the book. If they have seen the film they can compare the book and film. Which did they enjoy more? Why?
Comprehension	literal; inferential	Through the questions the children can empathise with the whales and record their feelings about the actions of the whalers.

Writing	discursive writing;
	drafting and redrafting
		Writing about various opinions
		    Throughout the Development books children have been asked to record their personal opinions about a variety of things, in some cases specifically looking at advantages and disadvantages. This work is developed here to look at discursive writing where an opinion is formed on the basis of facts. The stages to follow when producing factual writing are given along with the idea that writing needs an introduction and conclusion.
		    Facts regarding whale hunting are given for the children to consider. Discuss the difference between hunting for profit and why the Inuits hunt.

Stimulus	modern poetry	*The Song of the Whale* by Kit Wright.
Comprehension	inferential	While continuing the theme of the unit, the questions allow the children to consider purpose and audience, following on from the poems in Unit 8.
Personal choice		The options here are: 1 narrative writing; 2 poster; 3 discursive writing.

Answers

Comprehension – *Free Willy*

1 The dorsal fin cut the water like a knife would cut through something.
2 He would earn the money to buy a new boat.
3 He hopes the reader will see the whales as creatures who have a right to life rather than as so many pounds of whale meat which can be sold for profit.
4 the boat's engines
5 They banged the hull of the boat with their hands and sticks of wood.
6 Three Spots gave a long mournful squeal.
7 Individual answers.

Comprehension – *The Song of the Whale*

1 Individual answers suggesting that the poem is about the life of a whale who is in constant danger of being hunted and killed.
2 because of its fear of being killed and its grief for other whales who have been caught
3 Lipstick and polish are by-products of whale hunting.
4 Man would stop the singing of the whales by killing them.
5 Individual answers suggesting that the poet is concerned for the plight of the whale.
6 Individual answers suggesting that the poet wants the reader to feel sympathy and possibly outrage at the plight of the whales.

See also: **p. 58, Skills** notes.

Development Unit 10

Life in the factories

Development Book Aims:

1 To continue discursive writing.

2 To introduce the idea of summaries.

Teaching notes

Stimulus	factual text	"Life in the factories" from *Tools and Manufacturing* by Gordon Burne.
Comprehension	literal; inferential	**Reading for information** After the children have understood the details of the passage, they are asked for their opinion about the working conditions of children. Discuss the idea of children working. Would they rather be at work or in school? The children could read chapters 4 and 5 of *Oliver Twist*, where Oliver begins work with an undertaker.
Writing	summaries	**Writing a summary** This is the first time the children have been asked to summarise a passage. They have, however, had practice in making notes from factual sources. Encourage them to rely on their own notes and not to refer to the original when they are writing their summaries, and stress that their piece of work should be considerably shorter than the original. They can use the following passages from **Skills Book 5** for further practice: Unit 6, The watery planet; Unit 8, Night; Unit 9, Rainforests – what's the fuss about?; Unit 12, The great dinosaur mystery.
Stimulus	modern poetry	*Motor Cars* by Rowena Bennett, and *Cynddylan on a Tractor* by R S Thomas.
Comprehension	literal; inferential	**Machines – good or bad?** The questions on the two poems concentrate on the writers' attitudes to the respective machines. This forms the basis of the discursive writing to follow.
Writing	personal opinion; discursive writing	**Writing about opinions** Here the children are asked to choose a machine and research opinion as to the advantages and disadvantages of its invention. The children should make a list of the questions they want to ask. **Pcm 1** – Vehicles, will give them initial practice.
Personal choice		The options here are: 1 imaginative writing; 2 advertisement; 3 personal writing.

Answers

Comprehension – "Life in the factories"

1 1750 – no factories, people worked at home;
1850 – millions of people were working in factories.
2 Disadvantages for all: dangerous, dirty, worked 18 hours a day, many accidents, wages low.
Disadvantages for women: they could not be at home to look after children.

Disadvantages for children: had to start work at the age of 9, couldn't go to school.
3 They had to starve or steal or go to the workhouse.
4 Home life was poor; houses dark and airless; whole families in one room; no proper sanitation, water supply or rubbish collection; disease.
5 Individual answers.
6 to inform the reader

Comprehension – *Motor Cars*

1 The poet is high up and the cars look very small. They are moving slowly in lines and leave a 'muddy track' as insects sometimes do.
The noise they make from a distance sounds like the drone of bees. The beams from their headlights look like an insect's feelers.
2 The poet seems to be 'fond' of the motor cars and is interested in them.
3 Individual answers.

Comprehension – *Cynddylan on a Tractor*

1 He seems to have become part of the machine.
2 It scatters the hens and frightens the wildlife.
3 Individual answers suggesting that the purpose of the poem is to show that the tractor disturbs the normal life of the countryside and is out of place. The poet disapproves of the tractor.

name _____ date _____

Vehicles

These people have different opinions about vehicles.
Use what they are saying, and any ideas of your own, to write about
the advantages and disadvantages of vehicles.
Remember to think of a good introduction.
Remember to give your opinion in a conclusion based on the facts.

Moral tales

**Development Book
Aims:**

1 **To look at different versions
of the same story.**

2 **To introduce the idea of
fables.**

Teaching notes		
Stimulus	traditional tale	*The Blind Men and the Elephant.*
Comprehension	literal; inferential	**Reading for understanding** Once the children have understood the story they are asked to find the 'moral' i.e. what the story is trying to teach. Do they think stories are a good way of teaching? Do they know any stories from the Bible where Jesus was trying to teach the people?
Stimulus	traditional poetry	*The Blind Men and the Elephant* by John Godfrey Saxe. This is the same story written in verse.
Writing	comparisons – analysis; personal response	**Different versions** The children are asked to compare and contrast the two versions of the story and to record their own opinion of the strength of the point being made.
Stimulus	fables	**Aesop's fables** Do the children know any other fables? e.g. The Hare and the Tortoise; The Fox and the Grapes.
Writing	personal response	The children are required to read the fables and write what lesson each is trying to teach.

Writing	fables	**Writing your own fable**
		    The children are given guidance as to the point their fable may try to teach and the main elements they have to consider in this type of writing. For a first attempt they may like to work in pairs.
		    Consider some relevant problems which they might address through writing a fable, e.g. litter in the playground, danger on the road, etc.

Personal choice		The options here are: 1 play script, **pcm 1** – Play script planning sheet; 2 fable.

Answers

Comprehension – *The Blind Men and the Elephant*

1 He gathered the blind men together so that they could each examine the elephant.
2 They each touched only a part of the elephant, not the whole animal. They did not examine the elephant closely enough.

3 They each described only the part they had touched.
4 tongues like razors – very sharp, able to say hurtful things
to cut a long story short – to get to the point quickly
wild words – arguments
narrow view of every question – unable or unwilling to see another person's point of view

5 Individual answers suggesting that the prince was trying to teach the wise men to consider other people's opinions.
6 Individual answers.

name _____ date _____

Playscript planning sheet

Title

Scene Number	Setting	Characters

Development Unit 12

Mystery of the *Mary Celeste*

Development Book Aims:

1 **To continue looking at different types of narrative writing – mystery stories.**

Teaching notes		
Stimulus	factual text	**The Mystery of the *Mary Celeste*** This passage is suitable for a summary.
Comprehension	literal; inferential	**Reading for information** The questions require the children to look closely at the detail of the passage and to form their own conclusions. **Pcm 1** – Crossword, gives the children the opportunity to scan for information.
Writing	narrative – mystery stories	**Writing a mystery story** As with the preparation for other types of narrative writing, the notes guide the children through the things they need to think about and plan before starting the story. Emphasise that they have read a factual account and have to use this as a basis for a mystery story that will keep the reader in suspense. Discuss how they could do this, e.g. 1st person narrative – they could be the captain or the mate who went on board the *Mary Celeste*. 3rd person narrative – as the author, they can decide on the outcome of the mystery and give the readers clues at various points in the story.
Stimulus	traditional verse	*The Listeners* by Walter de la Mare. Continuing the idea of mysteries, this poem recounts a series of unusual events but makes no attempt to explain them.
Writing	personal response	**Poetry Study** The children do not have to answer the initial questions. They are there to show how the poem is built up and can be used as a basis for their paragraphs.
Personal choice		The options here are: 1 book cover/blurb writing; 2 factual report; 3 poetry.

Answers

Comprehension – "The Mystery of the *Mary Celeste*"

1 Atlantic
2 She was not following a definite course but going this way and that with the wind.
3 plenty of food and water; cargo intact in the hold
4 half-eaten breakfast; dead fire; half-finished calculation; chronometer was missing; cutlass smeared with blood; bloodstains on the deck rail; last entry in the log was ten days before
5 There was no sign of a struggle and nothing valuable had been taken.
6 Individual answers.

See also: **p. 70, Skills** notes.

name _____ date _____

Crossword

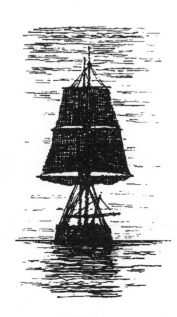

Across

3 Where the *Dei Gratia* was sailing to.

7 Where the *Dei Gratia* was sailing from.

9 Where the cargo was kept.

10 The name for the people who work on a ship.

11 It was smeared with blood.

Down

1 Daily events on board ship are recorded here.

2 He went aboard the *Dei Gratia*.

4 The cargo was found _____ .

5 The name of the strange ship.

6 Where the half finished calculation was found.

8 The *Mary Celeste* had been passing north of St. Mary's Island in the _____ .

Published by Thomas Nelson and Sons Ltd 1995

Development
Unit 13

Weird and wonderful

Development Book Aims:

1 To continue work on play scripts.

Teaching notes

Stimulus	modern fiction	"The Legend of Alderley" from *The Weirdstone of Brisingamen* by Alan Garner. This legend is told at the beginning of the book before the adventures of Colin and Susan in the present day. Suggest that the children read the book to see what happens and to find out the relevance of "The Legend of Alderley" to the children's adventures.
Comprehension	literal; inferential	The children are required to look carefully at the detail of the story and to use what they have learned about contrast in mystery stories to analyse the opening paragraphs of the legend.
Writing	play script	**Writing a play script** The children have tackled this type of work in earlier Development Books. Use **pcm 1** – The stage, for them to plan and make notes on stage settings. This work could be done in groups, each group taking a different setting.
Stimulus	traditional verse	*Jabberwocky* by Lewis Carroll.
Writing	personal response	**Poetry study** Despite the 'weirdness' of the vocabulary, it is not too difficult to make out what is happening in the poem. Children should have fun 'translating' the unusual words and this task can be continued in **Personal choice**, where they are asked to write two more verses to the poem where the Jubjub bird and the Bandersnatch are encountered!
Personal choice		The options here are: 1 narrative writing; 2 personal letter; 3 poetry.

Answers

Comprehension – "The Legend of Alderley"

1 He thought he would get a better price at the market.
2 Everyone admired the horse but nobody bought it.
3 The old man touched the rock with his staff, there was a noise like thunder, the horse reacted and the farmer fell off.
4 The light was gentle and soft rather than glaring.
5 The opening of the story is quite ordinary. The farmer is riding to market and we are given no indication that anything unusual is going to happen. The contrast comes with the sudden appearance of the old man.
6 The old man indicates that the sleeping knights will awaken when they are needed to protect the land from great danger.

Nelson

ENGLISH

DEVELOPMENT BOOK 5

Unit 13

Pcm 1

name _____   date _____

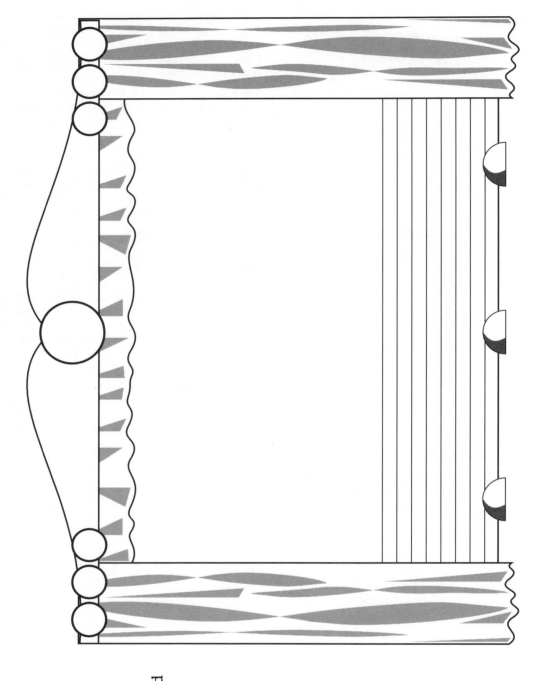

The stage

Use the diagram of the stage to draw the setting for one of the scenes in your play.

Make notes around the stage about:

colours;

materials;

where characters will enter and exit;

and anything else you think might be useful.

Use arrows to show the parts of the stage to which you are referring.

Development
Unit 14

1 To introduce the idea of prediction.

2 To introduce book reviews.

Teaching notes

Stimulus	modern fiction	*The Iron Man* by Ted Hughes. After the children have worked through the unit, suggest that they read the book to find out what happens. They may also like to read the sequel, *The Iron Woman*.
Comprehension	inferential	After each section of the story, the children are required to predict what they think might happen. Discourage them from reading on before they guess by stressing that there are no right and wrong answers. The author has chosen certain outcomes but others could be valid had he wanted his story to progress and end differently.
Writing	prediction	**Looking for clues** At each stage the children should make notes on the clues that would have helped them to predict the outcomes correctly. This type of exercise can be done with the opening paragraphs of many novels. **Pcm 1** – Prediction, gives the children some easy practice.
Writing	continuing a narrative	**Using the clues** Here the children are required to finish the first chapter using the clues. Discuss the characters – do some of the children see the hand and eyes as characters?
Stimulus	book reviews	The children were introduced to the concept of a book blurb at the end of **Development Book 4**. Here they are given guidance as to what should be included in a book review and are asked to analyse one for *The Iron Man*. Questions 1–6 can be used with reviews of other books and also to judge the book reviews they themselves write.
Writing	book reviews	**Writing your own book review** The children are required to choose a book they have enjoyed and write a book review. Additional guidance is given for non-fiction texts. The reviews could be illustrated and bound together as a class reference.
Personal choice		The options here are: 1 book cover/blurb writing; 2 conversation.

Answers

Writing – Looking for clues

1 The Iron Man 'swayed in the strong wind … he swayed forward'.
2 The Iron Man crashes down the cliff 'from rock to rock, snag to snag … And as he crashed and crashed and crashed'.

3 The fact that this is the first chapter and it is called The Coming of the Iron Man.
4 'Shiny, round and hard'.
5 'five legs'.
6 'Now the hand could see'.

Writing – Book reviews

1 The Iron Man.
2 Ted Hughes.
3 modern fairy story

4 children and adults
5 Individual answers.
6 likes the book very much

name _____   date _____

Predictions

Look at each pair of pictures.

1

Write what you think happens next.

_____

_____

2

Write what you think happens next.

_____

_____

3

Write what you think happens next.

_____

_____

Published by Thomas Nelson and Sons Ltd 1995

Development
Unit 15

Cats

Development Book Aims:

1 To show that the same subject can be treated in a variety of ways.

2 To revise various writing styles taught throughout the Development books.

Teaching notes		
Stimulus	factual text	**The cat family** An example of the theme of cats in factual writing, supported by illustration.
Comprehension	literal	Reading for information.
Stimulus	modern poetry	*Cat-Poem* by Joan Downar. An example of the theme of cats in poetic form.
Stimulus	traditional fiction	The Cheshire Cat from *Alice in Wonderland* by Lewis Carroll. An example of the theme of cats in narrative fiction.

Writing	comparisons – purpose and audience;
	Personal choice
		Revise the various **purposes** for which a piece may be written, e.g.
		    to inform;
		    to entertain;
		    to frighten;
		    to keep the reader in suspense;
		    to get across a particular point of view.
		Revise the various **audiences** for which a piece may be written, e.g.
		    for children;
		    for someone wanting to learn facts;
		    for people who like stories of different kinds;
		    for yourself;
		    for people you know;
		    for people you do not know.
		For each cat the children must decide:
		1 the purpose;
		2 the audience;
		3 the style (from the head of the cat);
		4 the elements in that kind of writing (from the body of the cat);
		5 how their work is going to be presented.

Personal choice		The whole of Unit 15 represents options for children's writing.

Answers

Comprehension – The cat family

1 ounce
2 dense woodlands
3 cheetah
4 jaguar
5 at night
6 cougar
7 grassland

See also: **p. 80, Skills** notes.
117

Nelson English
Skills Book 5
Record of Progress

Name: _____

Units

1 City life · 2 London life in Victorian times · 3 Centaurus I · 4 Lilliput · 5 The library puzzle · 6 The watery planet · 7 Jamaica Market · 8 Night · 9 Rainforests · 10 Machines and people · 11 World religions in the UK · 12 The great dinosaur mystery · 13 Dragons – fact or fiction? · 14 Cliffs under attack · 15 Lions – the cat facts

Skill	1	2	3	4	5	6	7	8	9	10	11	12	13	14	15	Comments
Unit completed/date																
comprehension	5 6	12	19	24	29 30	37	43 44	49	54	58 59	66	72	78	84	90	
vocabulary enrichment	7	12	20	24		38	45	49	55	60 61	66 67	72 74	78	84	90	
vocabulary choices	7	15			30	38	45									
nouns/pronouns	7				31	40	46				68					
verbs/tenses	7							50					79 80	87	90	
adjectives/adverbs	7	14			31				56				80			
phrases/clauses												73	80			
sentences	9								56			73 74		85	92	
paragraphs				26										85		
capital letters		13					45		57			74				
punctuation		13					45		57		67					
direct/indirect speech		13	20							61					91	
letters																
abbreviations/contractions					32								80	85		
dictionary/thesaurus				27		38						72		84		
adding ing/ed	9				33											
ous/ious																
ery/ary		14	21													
e + suffix	9															
y + suffix				27					57	61	69					
ll + suffix							47									
adding prefixes				25		41						75		86	93	
'tricky words'																
making plurals						41		51								
able/ible						41										
'i before e except …'													81			

Key

- ◩ 28   activity undertaken
- ◨⊠ 28   activity undertaken and understood
- ▨ 28   activity revisited and understood

118

Nelson English
Development Book 5
Record of Progress

Name: _____

Activity	1 City life	2 Victorian times	3 Do you believe in ghosts?	4 Other worlds	5 Advertising	6 The unsinkable Titanic	7 Jamaica	8 Night	9 Extinction!	10 Life in the factories	11 Moral tales	12 Mystery of the Mary Celeste	13 Weird and wonderful	14 Danger on the cliff	15 Cats	Comments
Unit completed/date																
literal comprehension	4/6	12	14	18	23	29	36	44	55	61	63/64	67	73	80	92	
inferential comprehension	4/6	9	14	18	23	32	36	44	49	55	59	61	67	73	80	94
descriptive writing	7	PC		21	23				48							96
research	9				37											
characterisation		10/11 14			37											
drafting and redrafting	7	14 15	19	24												
narrative		PC	PC	19	24	26										
conversation					26											
advertisements/poster					31	PC	PC	PC	PC	PC	PC	PC	PC			
factual	PC	PC	PC	PC	31	37	PC	PC								
imaginative			PC			37	45									
filling in forms							44									
persuasive writing							44									
business letter						46										
poetry									50	56						
discursive writing	PC		PC		PC			56	PC	62/63 64/65			PC	PC		
summary											69	71				
comparisons											69				95	
fables									45		71 PC					
personal response										46	69	77	83			
playscript											PC	81				
prediction														84 86		
book review														89		
personal	PC														95	
opinions		PC	PC	PC	PC	PC				PC		74 75	87	96		
book cover			PC	PC								PC	PC	PC		
diary			PC	PC												
personal letter		PC	PC													
interview																

Key

PC	Personal Choice assignment
☐ 28	activity undertaken
⊠ 28	activity undertaken and understood
◪ 28	activity revisited and understood

119

Thomas Nelson & Sons Ltd
Nelson House Mayfield Road
Walton-on-Thames Surrey
KT12 5PL UK

Nelson Blackie
Wester Cleddens Road
Bishopbriggs
Glasgow
G64 2NZ UK

Thomas Nelson Australia
102 Dodds Street
South Melbourne
Victoria 3205 Australia

Nelson Canada
1120 Birchmont Road
Scarborough Ontario
M1K 5G4 Canada

© John Jackman, Wendy Wren 1995

First published by
Thomas Nelson and Sons Ltd 1995

I(T)P   Thomas Nelson is an
         International Thomson Publishing Company
I(T)P   is used under licence

ISBN 0-17-424548-3
NPN 9 8 7 6 5 4 3 2 1

Printed in Great Britain
by Hobbs the Printers Ltd, Totton, Hampshire

Acknowledgements

The authors and publisher would like to thank the staff and pupils of the following schools, who have generously given their time to trial Nelson English. Their comments and criticisms have helped develop and polish the early concepts.

Ayr Grammar Primary School, Ayr
Beeston Primary School, Leeds
Caversham Primary School, Caversham, Reading
Cramond School, Cramond, Edinburgh
Fairfield Primary School, Basingstoke
Hampton Hill Junior School, Hampton Hill, Middlesex
Hampton Infants' School, Hampton, Middlesex
Holt Primary, Holt, Clwyd
Horndean Junior School, Hampshire
Lambton Primary School, Washington, Co. Durham
Laurel Bank School, Glasgow
Marlborough JMI School, Isleworth, Middlesex
Old Fleet Primary, Hull
St. Nicholas RC Combined School, Exeter
The Bocombra Primary School, Portadown,
Co. Armagh

We should also like to acknowledge the valuable advice and guidance received from our consultants:

Gervase Phinn, Senior General Inspector for English, North Yorkshire County Council
Patricia Gordon, Craigie College, University of Paisley

and from our teacher advisers:

Bill Ball, Maureen Barlin, Penny Bridgeland, Hilary Frost, Hilary Harriman, Roye Jackman, Sarah Lindsay, Isobel McGhee, Richard Painter, Mary Pereira, Liz Purvis, Pat Ranson, Andrea Samuels, Penny Seal, Eve Stephens and Tony D. Triggs.

The authors and publishers gratefully acknowledge the valuable contribution of the following documents:

National Curriculum (1995) England and Wales.

National Guidelines (Scotland) English Language 5 – 14.

Curriculum (Programmes of Study and Attainment Targets in English) Order (Northern Ireland) 1990.